T0319585

# Praise for *Project Management Nation*

"Jay does a fantastic job of applying proven project management processes and techniques to today's complex IT environment. His examples, charts, and overall approach provide a solid foundation to any IT project and project manager. A definite addition to the project manager's bookshelf!"

—Michael A. Brown, PMP, Senior Project Manager, Bank One Corp.

"No question, a must read for any IT project manager wanting to get involved with IT project management. Jason's down-to-earth approach makes a complicated subject easy to comprehend."

—Robert Fairchild, Project Manager, RCG Information Technology, NJ

"A sure path to success for any IT project! This book is concise and easy to read for anybody wanting to excel in IT project management."

—Dan Herbst, Software Engineer, Dallas, TX

"Jason's book provides real world project management insights for new as well as seasoned project managers. This is a comprehensive management primer, which distills the best practices for successfully navigating the current, turbulent IT business environment. It's witty, pragmatic and filled with vital lessons from actual situations."

—Arnold Pagan, PMP Project Manager, E-Business Deployment for Johnson & Johnson

"Jason has walked through the fires of project management and come out the other side. In this valuable book he shares the tools and techniques he's developed to ensure success in IT project delivery. Read it and improve your results."

—Rich Freedman, Author, *The IT Consultant* and *The eConsultant*

# PROJECT MANAGEMENT NATION

## tools, techniques, and goals for the new and practicing IT project manager

jason charvat

JOHN WILEY & SONS, INC

Copyright © 2002 by John Wiley & Sons, Inc., New York. All rights reserved.

No part of this publication may be reproduced, stored in a retrieval system or transmitted in any form or by any means, electronic, mechanical, photocopying, recording, scanning or otherwise, except as permitted under Sections 107 or 108 of the 1976 United States Copyright Act, without either the prior written permission of the Publisher, or authorization through payment of the appropriate per-copy fee to the Copyright Clearance Center, 222 Rosewood Drive, Danvers, MA 01923, (508) 750-8400, fax (508) 750-4470. Requests to the Publisher for permission should be addressed to the Permissions Department, John Wiley & Sons, Inc., 605 Third Avenue, New York, NY 10158-0012, (212) 850-6011, fax (212) 850-6008, E-Mail: PERMREQ@WILEY.COM.

This publication is designed to provide accurate and authoritative information in regard to the subject matter covered. It is sold with the understanding that the publisher is not engaged in rendering professional services. If professional advice or other expert assistance is required, the services of a competent professional person should be sought.

ISBN 0-471-13926-2

# Contents

# Foreword

More people work on IT (information technology) projects than on any other category of project. In fact, if you were to conduct a statistical investigation of who is doing what on projects implemented throughout the world, you would likely find that more people are working on IT projects than on all other types combined!

Until recently, those of us who have studied project management over the years have emphasized the universality of project issues encountered by project workers, regardless of the specific nature of the projects being undertaken. After all, a schedule is a schedule, whether it has been created for a construction project, an FDA approval effort, or a software development undertaking. Thus, it is possible to learn key scheduling tools without worrying about the specific context in which the schedule occurs. Similar arguments can be made about budget and resource allocation tools.

Without question, it is remarkable how the experiences of people working on different types of projects are so similar. When construction project managers get together with software project managers, they find that they have many common experiences to share. For example, to the extent that both groups use borrowed resources (called *matrix management*), they face the common situation where project managers do not control the resources with which they must work. And they both operate in environments where there is a tendency for project scope to grow as the project is carried out (called *scope creep*).

With the onset of the new millennium, we have begun to turn our attention to the special circumstances governing project work in different business areas. In particular, we now recognize that knowledge-based projects face a different set of challenges than the challenges that traditional projects in the construction and defense industries encounter. For example, knowledge-based projects are heavily oriented toward dealing with intangibles. Knowledge itself is ephemeral and ever-changing. Because knowledge is abstract, it is hard to capture and articulate customer needs and to convert these into concrete requirements. These are the types of issues that workers on knowledge-based projects must contend with day by day.

In *Project Management Nation,* Jason P. Charvat deals explicitly with the challenges faced by project professionals working on IT projects. He begins by recognizing that the key players on IT projects are different from those encountered on other types of projects. For IT projects to succeed, for example, it is important to have them supported by senior level *project sponsors.* IT projects without powerful and attentive sponsors are projects that are likely to encounter a host of difficulties. Also, because IT projects are concerned with converting business needs into technical solutions, project teams must be comprised of a wide range of players reflecting both the business and technical dimensions of the project effort.

Charvat also recognizes that IT projects must conform to the *system development life cycle* (SDLC). SDLCs have emerged over the years as ways to handle the inherent complexity of knowledge-based systems. They are the engines that drive the project, and a key challenge of IT project managers is to plan projects that operate in harmony with the SDLC. Throughout his book, Charvat discusses project management in the SDLC context.

Charvat also acknowledges that conventional project management practice has a significant role to play in IT project management. In the second half of the book, where he discusses project planning, control, and closure, he reviews standard project management techniques in the areas of scheduling and configuration control. But even here, he puts an IT spin on the material, as when he highlights the special role of testing in software development.

This book serves a bridging function, where best-practice IT management and conventional project management merge. By addressing the special issues associated with IT projects, it offers IT project managers pertinent insights that they would not encounter in the standard project management literature.

J. Davidson Frame, PhD
Dean, University of Management
and Technology
Arlington, VA USA

# Preface

This book is a usable and practical approach on the subject of IT project management. The title of the book — *Project Management Nation* — was largely intended to illustrate the point that project managers at times approach IT projects in similar ways. They could thus be seen as a nation of professionals, irrespective of where they reside globally. The chapters presented to you have been carefully structured and the intent is for you to accomplish the following goals: first, to immediately benefit from the knowledge, and second, to apply this knowledge from a information technology perspective. The chapters appear in a logical manner and should be read sequentially to gain understanding of the concepts and techniques. By understanding one chapter, you will be able to start one phase of a project during its life cycle. By mastering all, you will be able to participate or actively engage in completing all phases of a project. This book consists of nine chapters that are independent, yet all connected:

> ➤ *Chapter 1: Understanding Project Strategy.* I am writing this chapter primarily for the project sponsor or executive team in order to detail the business and IT strategy issues, their relationships to projects, and, more importantly, the manner in which project management actually relates to this organizational

strategy. Without a clear strategy, it is not apparent why projects are important to a business, and, as a result, many projects are either cancelled or face bitter consequences later on.

➤ *Chapter 2: Becoming an IT Project Manager.* During this chapter, I identify what makes one project manager better than the next, by evaluating the attributes, characteristics, and type of person that makes an effective project manager.

➤ *Chapter 3: Project Concepts.* I consider why a formal life cycle approach works best in the project management environment, as many businesses all have their own project methodologies and approaches. This chapter examines which one is better suited to a specific project.

Once giving a complete explanation as to how the overall strategy drives project management, the book moves on to Chapters 4 to 9. These chapters focus on what you, as the project manager, need to do with your project team and stakeholders to ensure that the project goals are achieved and that the business benefits are delivered.

➤ *Chapter 4: The Project Analysis.* This chapter identifies and concentrates specifically on how and when a project actually starts. Do project managers simply jump in and run with the project or are there some formalities to consider before planning the project? Within this chapter I show the feasibility of a project right through to the approval of the project.

➤ *Chapter 5: Planning for Success.* Planning a project can be demanding for any project manager who has never attempted to perform such a task. This chapter deals with the basic essentials of planning a project. Simply put, many project failures that occur today are due to failure of planning and estimation. This chapter presents ways to overcome these failures.

➤ *Chapter 6: Executing the Project.* In this chapter I present how to execute a project with the project stakeholders, not forgetting the issues and pitfalls that need to be addressed during this phase.

➤ *Chapter 7: Controlling the Project.* Controlling any project requires essential project management skills and techniques. This chapter examines how to control a project smoothly and in a timely manner during the various project phases.

➤ *Chapter 8: Implementing the Project.* Within this chapter I identify and recognize the most important areas of project implementation. To implement a project based solely on a gut feeling is not good enough. Most of the failures that occur today are failures of implementation!

➤ *Chapter 9: Closing the Project.* Within this chapter I specifically explore the practical requirements and issues that need to be catered to by the project manager when completing a project.

This book is intended to be of significant interest to both the new and practicing IT project managers who are primarily interested in starting a IT project once they have been identified or have been assigned a project by management. Knowing which key areas and templates are needed and understanding what to do during each project phase (with the help of valuable project lessons learned) will go a long way in establishing your credibility as a project manager. To avoid any surprise on your part, let me state that my intention with this book was not to delve into the great depths of each knowledge area and technique (such as PERTS and Gantt charts), but rather to supplement it from a practicing perspective. I welcome any critique you may have.

Let me conclude by insisting that we who are responsible for managing projects must do so with such uniqueness and diligence as to ensure that project management will continue to be seen as the key differentiator by which organizations want to deliver products and solutions. This publication is based on my experience, valuable client input, and discussions held with fellow project managers. The opinions expressed in this book are those of the author and do not necessarily represent those of RCG Information Technology, Inc. I hope that you will enjoy the manner in which this book is presented, with its logic, useful facts, findings, and applications for everyday IT project management.

# Acknowledgments

I would like to recognize the support of the management team at RCG Information Technology, Inc., who provided me with an environment in which to apply myself. I would like to thank Gary Hau for helping me solve the many detailed IT development issues one needs to consider when managing complex IT projects. My gratitude is extended to Dr. J. Davidson Frame from the University of Management and Technology in Washington, D.C., for his discussions and opinions on the field of project management. Thanks go to Matthew Holt, senior editor at John Wiley & Sons. To Bob Fairchild and Rick Freedman, thanks for your insight and reviews. To all those people that have contributed to the publication of this book, I thank you collectively. Lastly, special thanks go to my wife Liesl and son Matthew, who have kept my life so organized during all these years.

# Chapter *1*

# Understanding Project Strategy

## ■ PROJECT STRATEGY IN MOTION

Sometimes all this talk of business strategy, competitive edge, and technology gets a little hard to digest all at once. In the course of my work as a project consultant, I notice on a daily basis how rapidly computer software and technologies change, and it's getting difficult to keep up. Before you know it, another version of software is being introduced or a newer technology is on the market. Today, you can get state-of-the-art software applications that can be developed far more quickly than before, allowing organizations improved functionality and greater opportunities. Senior executives face the frontline, constantly bombarded by software companies and consultants who market information technology (IT) solutions that are able to revolutionize and improve their organizations. Sadly, not many of these software systems get developed or implemented to the extent that the client would have liked. The most important predictor of an organization's ultimate success or failure is the strategy that it chooses to adopt.

These organizations are challenged, as they need to keep pace with competitive markets, client needs, and

1

marketplace trends. Winning is basically about who has the upper hand (either with new technology or quicker implementations): The only winners will be those executives who are able to reinvent their companies quickly enough to take full advantage of the efficiencies and better distribution that new technologies can offer. To overcome their competition and to be an industry leader, companies need to be able to provide their clients the latest products and available services. And project management plays an important role in all of this.

However, getting to the point of introducing a product or solution requires strategic assessment and planning, which must be done before anything can even commence. The senior executive team within the organization needs to come up with a strategic plan (or game plan, to use a sports metaphor) before any engagement takes place. Without a strategic plan in place, executives can literally move from one solution offering to the next, spending millions of dollars in the process, with the result being that many projects head south. The point, after all, is to make sure the organization is more valuable, has a business strategy in place, and is ready to start with this game plan.

From project management's point of view, there is no need to manage any project if the project manager has no idea why it's being done in the first place. It's crucial for any project manager to address the larger issues of the business strategy and see where the project fits in the overall framework. It isn't easy—but it needs to be done. The thoughts contained within this chapter are important, as they represent the strategic concepts and ideas formulated at the corporate or business level and the role of the project manager at a lower functional or operating level. When I address business strategy, I am also including the alignment of information technology as an integral part of the game plan. The reason may be that companies that are reluctant to invest in new technologies may therefore never address their IT problems, or worse, are left behind by their competitors. Therefore, every organization needs a documented strategy that is realistic and is agreed to by everyone. Good strategy leads to good results. Bad strategy will not allow an organization to survive its competition.

Let me illustrate an example of how technology and market trends are forcing organizations to adapt their business strategies to meet future IT demands. It is estimated that by 2005 over 80 million people will be sending wireless images on the fly, using numerous digital devices. Sounds like something from Star Trek, doesn't it? If this prediction comes true, then existing network infrastructures run the serious risk of becoming outdated, as newer high-speed networks on the 128 kbps and 384K Time Multiple Access Division (TDMA) range will be needed to handle these technologies. Many companies will therefore need to revise their business and IT strategies, and project managers will be required to implement these resulting new strategies (see Figure 1.1).

## ➤ Achieving Company Strategy

The first and most important step in achieving a company strategy is developing and setting in motion a business strategy for the organization. The IT strategy then forms the core part of how to get there; therefore, when IT is involved, these strategies must be verified and discussed at an executive level. If the overall strategy is wrong or the problem strategically misunderstood, the results are, not surprisingly, less than satisfactory. No amount of effort or leadership or tactical brilliance from the executive officers will compensate for an incorrect strategy. Strategies are always formed and executed at different levels within any organization. Table 1.1 illustrates those levels where project managers contribute the most to the overall strategy.

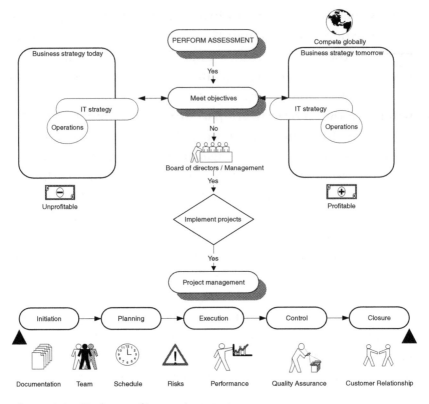

**Figure 1.1** Understanding project strategy

The functional strategy level refers specifically to the game plan for a particular business activity, department, or business process. The primary role of the functional strategy is to support the company's overall strategy and competitive approach. The operational strategy deals with how to manage costs, quality targets, and delivery at the frontline. Many companies use project management to deliver strategic goals and actions. Companies are now realizing that in the fast-paced Information Age, weapons such as speed, opportunities, and niches are prized elements in any business arsenal. In all subsequent chapters in this book, I focus on how project managers ensure that strategy succeeds

**Table 1.1**  Strategy levels within organizations

| Strategy Levels | Large Enterprises | Small Business |
|---|---|---|
| Corporate | ✓ | |
| Business | | ✓ |
| Functional | ✓ | ✓ |
| Operational | ✓ | ✓ |

at both the functional and operational levels. Clearly, there is a need to understand something about strategy after all.

Information technology is changing at such an amazing rate that, in order for companies to survive in the competitive marketplace, they must use more and more solutions that require enhancing existing systems and de-commissioning older ones. So, too, project management needs to fit into the overall company strategic model, whereby project management is the area that brings in the IT solutions (products or services) before competitors can react. Applying project management and understanding the strategic intent of the company justifies maneuvering the competitive advantage correctly, which is all the more important. Projects need to bring in solutions that not only are faster, cheaper, or have a unique, focused cost advantage, but also are able to serve clients world-wide.

Sun Tzu, a famous military general, once said

*The one with many strategic factors on his side wins. . . .*
*The one with few strategic factors on his side loses. In*
*this way, I can tell who will win and who will lose.*

The project manager has to take the slog up the mountain and ask the project sponsor and other stakeholders tough questions such as, "How do we measure success at the end of this project?", "What do you really want to buy for all this money we're going to spend?" To get answers to these

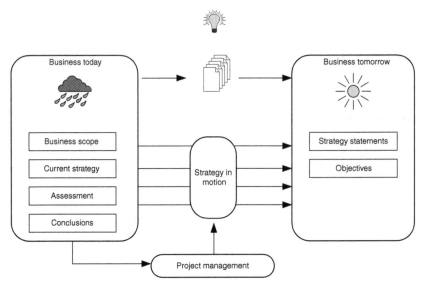

**Figure 1.2** Project management involvement in formulating strategies

questions, everyone must examine the strategic aspect, which starts at the very beginning of the project idea or concept. Without an understanding of the desired result, the project manager cannot fend off scope creep and define success for the people who will be doing the work (see Figure 1.2).

## ➤ Purpose of Strategy

The purpose of strategy is to provide direction and concentration of effort as organizations continually strive to improve their position or gain the upper hand within the marketplace. Basically, it's a struggle for advantage, and the one with the best advantage wins. It's that simple. On what areas must businesses concentrate? Businesses clearly have to

➤ Gain new advantages that increase or improve customer satisfaction, which will differentiate them from their competitors

➤ Either eliminate or minimize their competitors

➤ Achieve speed to market

➤ Re-engineer business processes for improved competitiveness

➤ Align their organizations to the latest economic trends

➤ Implement the strategy (i.e., through projects)

➤ Evaluate the success of the strategy (i.e., measure project success)

Organizations must focus on project management as the key business driver that will achieve these advantages for them. As a profession, project management would be able to support the overall business strategy with clear-cut benefits and advantages.

1. *Reduce delivery costs.* Project management can provide products and services more cheaply by following a structured and formalized project methodology and by ensuring that excessive costs are not spent without due consideration.

2. *Enable quicker product to market.* The advantage permits the business to deliver products or services more efficiently than the competitors and the business is able to react more favorably to market demands.

3. *Focus advantage.* The projects will be focused more on the client needs and products, instead of having a solution that does not deliver the expected returns.

4. *Produce quality deliverables.* Project management builds quality into the products or services right from

the start, ensuring that the right things are developed at the right specification.

5. *Provide customer advantage.* Project management gains advantages for their organization by working together with the customer(s) and by accommodating their needs and requirements.

So, to gain a competitive advantage, executives will inevitably ask certain questions: (1) Do we have the resources and skills to gain the advantage? (2) Is it worth the effort for us to do this? (3) How long would it take for us to gain the advantage? (4) Who within our business will take charge of leading the development of a new product or services? (5) How compatible is the solution with the rest of our existing IT portfolio? (6) How much would it cost us to gain the advantage? (7) What is it that we want to do with the technology?

## ➤ Strategic Leadership

All companies require that the overall strategy be driven from the top of the company in order for projects to be successful. The organizational executive team usually provides the leadership for the overall business and IT strategy. Before any project is even considered, the executive team must assess and align the solution against the business and IT strategy, before committing any project resources to it. Companies can achieve this by formulating a strategy steering committee, which is responsible for deciding on the priority and feasibility of each and every project within the organization.

The source of many failed projects can be traced to the point where corporate politics gets involved, and executives often throw big money at technologies to solve their problems. Project managers are accordingly assigned to such projects, and, eventually, they fail. The IT project should therefore complement the overall business strategic plan. Once the steering committee has deemed that the strategy is satisfactory, the following tactics may be necessary to implement this strategy:

➤ Executives may need to establish alliances or cooperation agreements with other businesses or competitors. Synergy is the name of the game here. The sum is greater than the parts. If strategic alliances are formed, the project manager will need to work across all environments and consider using soft skills such as (1) people management, (2) negotiation, (3) presentations, (4) diplomacy, and (5) tact.

➤ Additionally, organizations often need to reshape their structures to accommodate subtle changes to already-established strategies. This is why it is so common to read about companies restructuring in the business media.

➤ Organizations need to have available resources (i.e., project managers, facilities, etc.) to execute the various projects that have been identified as a result of the strategy work session. Sometimes, attempting too many projects all at once in an effort just to remain competitive can result in failure. An example of this is trying to integrate multiple IT projects concurrently with an existing billing system. It is better to implement a few successful projects instead of several projects, many of which may not succeed.

## ➤ Executive Responsibilities

Ultimately, the core functions of executives are to craft, implement, and execute strategy. Period. They craft strategies in order to (1) shape their company's course of action and (2) coordinate a company-wide game plan. Project managers should obtain the approval and "go-ahead" of the executive team for all IT project engagements, thus ensuring that the appropriate processes for the delivery of the business and IT have been scrutinized, reviewed, and prioritized. Executives and project managers should agree on the following objectives:

➤ Alignment of the proposed IT investment plan (i.e., projects) with the company business objectives;

➤ Commitment to delivery of measurable business benefits within schedule, cost, and risk that are realistic and appropriate to the business;

➤ A shared understanding of the responsibilities for delivery of the project between system users and the IT specialists;

➤ A plan to benchmark the performance of existing processes in business terms and to track improvements;

➤ Risk management that recognizes the need to accommodate change.

It is common practice in many companies to appoint both a business project manager and a marketing manager to deliver the business benefits and to appoint an IT project manager to deliver the information system or solution. These managers should be held accountable to the company for the success of the project. In companies with an on-going IT investment program, the executive team should ensure that these processes are being systematically planned, executed, and reviewed.

**Table 1.2** Uniquenesses between operations project and program management

| Operation Management | Project Management | Program Management |
|---|---|---|
| Repeated | Unique | Can be both |
| Continuous | Temporary | Can be both |
| Evolutionary | Revolutionary | Can be both |
| Stable resources | Varying Resources | Can be neither |
| Focus on products | Focus on Products | Focus on benefits |
| | Focus on Solutions | |

## ➤ Understanding Project, Program, and Operations

Today, the majority of clients require project managers to formulate the conceptual thinking necessary for planning the entire project. Not too surprisingly, the inclination of most project managers is to skip the strategic phase of project management and to start the project. It is essential that project managers understand the key differences between how companies do business, in order to best achieve project success (see Table 1.2).

## ➤ What are Strategic Projects?

Where the project is a component of a broader business sense, it should be assessed as an integral part of the strategic program. All the normal financial assessment rules should be applied. The executive team should pay close attention to those parts of the proposed solution that clearly show the benefits of proceeding with the solution. Managers should ensure that detailed plans for achieving the benefits, and specific responsibility for delivering them, are in place.

IT planning must take account of the intended direction of the business, financial constraints and criteria, and human resource (HR) plans and policies. It must also be flexible enough to cope with any likely response from competitors over the whole project life cycle. Project managers should have a clearly communicated policy for the way to collect, use, and store information in support of the business objectives and the way the systems will enable them to harness the value of this information in the future.

## ➤ Translating Strategy into Projects

Once the strategy has been determined and has been approved by the company executive team, the responsibility of the project success does not fall only at the feet of the project manager. The chief executive officer (CEO), chief information officer (CIO), directors, functional management, and staff all have specific tangible and intangible roles in the project. In this manner, mutual expectations can be met and benefits realized. For a successful transition from strategy to project, the business must have in place

- ➤ Agreement on what needs changing, and why (this should be clearly supported by the project sponsor);

- ➤ A common "language" for analyzing and describing requirements, based on a shared understanding of the business processes across "client," purchasing, and information systems (IS) departments (don't assume this is the case);

- ➤ Agreed processes that involve the users in the selection and design of systems solutions (consider making a "client," rather than an IS specialist, the program manager responsible for delivering the business benefits);

- ➤ The support of a skilled, experienced technology project manager.

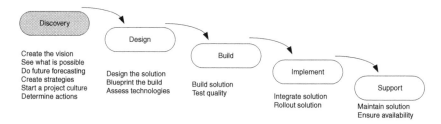

**Figure 1.3**   The basic beginnings of strategy on a project life cycle

Each and every project should have some sort of a mission. The *mission* identifies the client's requirements and clearly defines the purpose of the project. A project's mission must be completed for success of the project. *Objectives* define the success criteria for the project. The objectives relate directly to the completion of the project's mission. Completing all of the objectives should accomplish the project's mission. Measurable objectives provide a method of quantifying the results and establishing quality standards to evaluate the success of the project. Figure 1.3 illustrates the need for strategic thinking on a typical project.

## ➤ Strategic Requirements

It is essential that the results of the project analysis be captured, as a formal expression of business needs. Specifying business requirements from a strategic perspective is not easy and it demands considerable skill, creativity, and breadth of vision. Additionally, having the necessary experience and knowledge of the specific business environment assists executives in formulating the strategy. If this cannot be performed, managers may want to consider using an independent, objective third party that has demonstrated its capability in prior strategy engagements. This third party is basically brought in by an executive team to facilitate and help document business requirements. There are significant advantages to this, and many organizations are even working in this way with strategic alliance partners as well. It encourages shared-risk and partnership-style relationships.

The majority of company staff will have a limited understanding of business strategy (let alone IT strategy) as it is a difficult art to master. The following suggestions will assist executives and project managers alike in attaining some perspective on strategy.

➤ Attend conferences and seminars on strategy.

➤ Join professional associations.

➤ Read publications on strategy.

➤ Have a mentor.

➤ Study and practice.

### ➤ Senior Management Commitment

A mutually acceptable commitment between a project sponsor and a project team must exist before a viable project exists. A project sponsor is a knowledgeable person who represents the eventual owner of the product of the project and who is responsible for providing the necessary resources (money, goods, services, and general direction, as appropriate). A project team is a knowledgeable and qualified group able and willing to undertake the work of the project. A mutually acceptable commitment is one in which there is agreement on the goals and objectives of the project in terms of the product's scope, quality grade, time to completion, and final cost. Effective and efficient policies and procedures must be in place for the conduct of the project commitment. Such policies and procedures must cover, at a minimum, clear roles and responsibilities, delegation of authority, and processes for managing the scope of work, including changes, maintenance of quality, and schedule and cost control.

## ➤ Executive Requirements on Strategy

Project managers need to realize that executives within organizations are big on making things happen. Without a doubt, they are totally results-orientated. Due to their positions (i.e., CEO, CIO, director, etc.) they are held accountable to their shareholders for "results." Because of this, executives tend to identify and focus on those projects that contribute to the following:

- ➤ Keeping the shareholders happy
- ➤ Increasing the market share
- ➤ Raising revenues
- ➤ Attracting new clients
- ➤ Getting higher dividends
- ➤ Lowering any operational expenses
- ➤ Increasing the efficiency in the company
- ➤ Increasing repeat client visits
- ➤ Lowering the cost of sales
- ➤ Making workers more productive and having a satisfied employee workforce

Therefore, executives are big on specific, demonstrable progress and measurable results, and if project managers cannot guarantee any visible return on these factors, they can more than likely expect minimal sponsorship on their projects and even a dip in their careers.

## ➤ Understanding the Cultural Environment

An informed management must provide a supportive cultural environment that will enable the project team to produce its best work. An informed management is one that understands the project management process. A supportive cultural environment is one in which the project is clearly backed by executives and management; it is also one that allows project teams to produce their best work without unnecessary bureaucratic hindrance. Following this principle means that executives and management need to align the project manager's leadership and management style to both the type of project and its complexity.

## ➤ The Project Charter

The project charter is developed as a precursor to the commencement of formal activity relating to a project. It took me many years to fully understand what the actual purpose of the project charter was. It represented yet another process document—an administrative burden. It seemed to me that I was merely duplicating project information in virtually every single document I was producing. Surely, I only needed a project plan to gain approval for the project.

The charter is basically prepared in order to describe, to executive management, the requirements and overview for the proposed project, and it is the primary document used by executive management to approve the necessary resources (work-hours and budget) for the pending project. The bottom line is that even if the project is short in length, develop a charter. It gives some credibility to the upcoming project and also gives the writer of the charter credibility as the chosen project manager. These people are the people who endorse the project. Isn't it amazing how much more smoothly a project flows with an executive on board!

Without a project charter, staff throughout the company will never be able to see the importance of the project in the same light as the project manager does, due to the fact that they are uninformed and they are often uncertain as to who is supporting the effort. This project may appear to be just another one that is taking place. However, if the company is aware of the CEO's commitment to the project, the project manager will be amazed at the positive reaction and response received during the entire project process.

When the project charter has been completed, the ideal situation is for the project manager to personally deliver the project charter to the executive's office for approval. Once the charter has been delivered, the project manager should make a call three days after the executive gets the project charter, in order to follow-up on progress. That allows one day for the charter to go through the executive's internal mail system and two days for the executive to review the charter. By personally getting involved, the project manager shows a commitment to the project and demonstrates a positive approach to the process (see Figure 1.4).

## ➤ Effective Communication

Many projects are instigated from the top down and project managers are accordingly appointed to take charge of a project. Senior executives rarely misguide staff, are very upfront, and would rather not see the project manager wasting anyone's time in their company. Therefore, a dynamic communication channel should exist between the project sponsor and the project manager for all decisions affecting the project. I have found this to be the most powerful way of achieving project success. This principle is necessary for the effective and efficient administration of the project commitment. The project manager must have the skills, experience, dedication, commitment, authority, and tenacity to

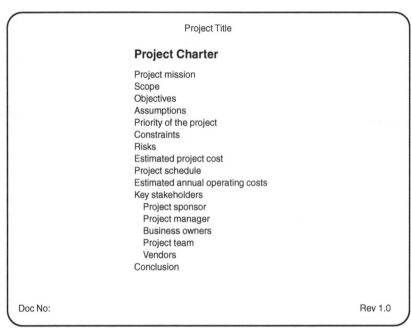

Project Title

**Project Charter**

Project mission
Scope
Objectives
Assumptions
Priority of the project
Constraints
Risks
Estimated project cost
Project schedule
Estimated annual operating costs
Key stakeholders
   Project sponsor
   Project manager
   Business owners
   Project team
   Vendors
Conclusion

Doc No:                                                                            Rev 1.0

**Figure 1.4**  The origination of the charter

lead the project to success, and must know how to deal with executives on the project level.

Motivating senior executives to understand the need for the project may not be for everyone! But one thing is certain: The project manager should be the single point of contact, both for submitting the project for review and negotiating its approval—not anyone else! If the project manager cannot present and communicate the project at an executive level, then someone else should be running the project. If a project manager is able to communicate well, then he or she has a great shot at a fantastic career in project management.

# ■ DEVELOPING THE STRATEGIC PLAN

The following section lays out a strategic plan for a software company. It reviews strengths, weaknesses, opportunities, and threats (known collectively as "SWOT"); A technique which allows project stakeholders to list important or significant areas relating to the project; presents a series of statements relating to the company's vision, mission, values, and objectives; and sets out its proposed strategies and goals through project management. This format is typical.

## ➤ Developing the Strategic SWOT Analysis

Table 1.3 shows a strategic plan that addresses the following key strengths, weaknesses, opportunities, and threats for Company xx, Inc.

## ➤ Vision

The vision for Company xx, Inc., in two years time is:

> *Company xx, Inc., will have annualized sales of $30 million and be profitable. It will employ 2,000 consultants who are mainly engaged in E-solutions, marketing, sales, and project management. Company xx, Inc., will offer five core solutions and provide added-value services to a large client base throughout the continental United States and two countries overseas. Our solutions will be technically advanced and will be tailored where necessary to offer advantages and improvements over our competitors' possible offerings. We will continue to expand through organic growth and acquisitions in related technology and market segments.*

### Mission Statement

The primary focus of Company xx, Inc., is defined as:

**Table 1.3**  Company xx, Inc., SWOT analysis

| Strengths | Weaknesses |
| --- | --- |
| Key client acquired | Lack of awareness about prospective client |
| Initial solution can evolve into range of offerings | Need additional IT staff for delivery team |
| Located near a major corporate HQ | Emerging new technologies |
| Very focused management/staff | Need aggressive account executive placed at client |

| Opportunities | Threats |
| --- | --- |
| Client owns many companies— diverse markets | Could attract major competition |
| Possible off-shore development | Economy turbulent—affecting sales of IT systems |
|  | Emerging technology could threaten solution |

*We will design, develop, and market advanced E-solutions for our clients. These web-based systems work with specialist hardware supplied by major integrators. Our solutions are distinguished from our competitions' by their sophisticated interfaces, scalability, and ease of modification and implementation. Sales are made directly and through our Sales and Marketing channels established in the continental United States and overseas markets.*

### Corporate Values

The corporate values governing development will include the following:

➤ Company xx, Inc., operates in accordance with the highest standards in all relationships with clients, suppliers, the environment, and the community.

➤ Company xx, Inc., fosters a climate that encourages innovation and diligence among staff and rewards accordingly.

### Business Objectives

Longer-term business objectives of Company xx, Inc., are summarized as

➤ Expanding the business aggressively and offering above-average returns to shareholders

➤ Becoming the leading innovative e-solutions company within the five core solutions areas

## ➤ Key Strategies

Company xx, Inc., will pursue the following critical strategies:

➤ Extend the current core technical solution areas.

➤ Intensify senior management team in sales/marketing.

➤ Strengthen human resources function and develop a Career Development Program.

➤ Seek new market segments for solutions.

The company will also pursue the following important strategies:

➤ Start participating in international trade shows and activities.

➤ Develop overseas market entry plans.

➤ Pursue strategic alliances with our core technologies.

➤ Strengthen and promote web presence.

➤ Seek new market segments and applications for our solutions and services.

## Major Goals

The following key targets will be achieved by Project ABC over the next two years:

➤ Achieve IT solution sales of $9 million by 200X.

➤ Report annualized profits of $2.5 million in 200X.

➤ Establish Company xx to be the largest solution provider by 200X.

➤ Become largest supplier of customized IT systems in four countries within 200X.

➤ Employ 200 technically qualified IT staff by 200X.

## Strategic Action Programs

The following strategic action programs will be implemented:

➤ *CEO and President* will, within five months, prepare comprehensive business plan.

➤ *Chief finance officer (CFO)* will, within three months, introduce an improved cost reporting solution.

➤ *Marketing senior vice president* will, within six months, implement new client relationship model to strengthen sales and marketing function in all xx states.

➤ *Solutions senior vice president* will, within six months, identify and align company solutions to industry demands and pursue technical alliances.

➤ *Regional account managers* will, within two months, develop and implement accelerated market entry and will develop plans of products and services.

## ■ DEVELOPING THE PROJECT STRATEGY

The success of any project is achieved by ensuring that the correct strategy and focus have been assigned to the respective project. Many companies fail to identify and prioritize their projects properly. The result is that no one assesses the company portfolio of projects, and many projects fail because of that. Some key elements that need to be addressed when strategizing and aligning projects to the overall business are

➤ Understanding the need for the project

➤ Ensuring the company strategy is correctly aligned to the project

➤ Finding the right sponsor or champion for the project

➤ Having a project charter

➤ Being able to fund the project

Figure 1.5 represents a typical list of projects within a company. It is essential that a priority list be developed for the senior executive level prior to any project commencing.

Sun Tzu said

*When your strategy is deep and far reaching, then what you gain by your calculations is much, so you can win before you even fight. When your strategic thinking is shallow and near-sighted, and then what you gain by your calculations is little, so you will lose before you do*

Project Title

**Project Prioritization List—July**

| Project Name | Department | Pr. | Estimate | Contact |
|---|---|---|---|---|
| Web Migration | E-Commerce | 4 | $108K | J. Wang |
| Billing Upgrade v3.0 | Finance | 2 | $989K | P. Raut |
| UML Rollout | IT | 1 | $180K | G. Hau |
| Imaging Front-end* | IT | 1 | $220K | M. Genovese |
| Workflow Manager | IT | 1 | $120K | N. Johnson |
| Career Manager v1.0 | HR | 3 | $270K | M. Christie |
| LDAP Replacement | IT | 1 | $89K | J. Archer |
| iStore Project | Sales | 3 | $300K | D. Robus |
| Project Aspen | Marketing | 5 | $45K | B. Coole |
| Acquisition Reporter | Procurement | 4 | $7K | J. Brown |
| Project Risk Tool | PSO | 4 | $43K | J. Crown |
| Configurator v3.0 | IT | 2 | $55K | L. Cole |
| Financial Report PII | Finance | 1 | $360K | TBA |

*Imaging rollout project cannot be started due to the software availability—4 month lead time

**Figure 1.5**   The prioritization of your project portfolio

*battle. Much strategy prevails little strategy, so those with no strategy cannot help but be defeated. Therefore it is said that victorious warriors win first and then go to war, while defeated warriors go to war first, and then seek to win.*

## ➤ I Wish I Had Known That

It is often important to understand where other projects went wrong in order to avoid facing those problems again. To better ensure the success of a project, the project manager should remain aware of the following issues:

➤ The delivery of business benefits must remain a senior-level priority throughout the project.

➤ Remain focused on measuring the business improvements — measuring can make them happen.

➤ Benefits come from exploitation by the system owners and users. Allow enough time to prepare and train them, or they will not be able to exploit the system effectively.

➤ Project managers should recognize that, in addition to the expected benefits, they need to allow for other benefits to emerge, as the capability of the new system becomes better understood.

➤ Installing a new solution achieves nothing on its own. Do not expect the supplier to deliver the business benefits.

➤ At the end of each project, conduct an independent review to confirm that planned benefits have been realized and that the lessons learned are recorded and applied to future projects.

➤ Focus on the business benefits, then the technological ones.

➤ Project managers should only approve projects when they are confident that the projects support business objectives, and they should then make the support public. Senior management sponsorship is vital.

➤ Plan to achieve measurable improvements.

➤ Don't "leave it to the professionals." If a project manager delegates responsibility for the management of a project or program, it must be to someone who is accountable to the Board for delivering the business benefits.

➤ Plan sufficient resources for training.

➤ Review projects to confirm that planned benefits are being realized.

## ■ LESSONS LEARNED FOR UNDERSTANDING PROJECT STRATEGY

Lessons learned that apply to business strategy fall into the domain of the senior executives, as most strategic decisions are made within this group. Some of the immediate lessons executives may learn include the following:

➤ CEOs insist on a project being carried out because they want it done. These approaches are often successful; however, there are just as many projects that fail to get off the ground, as these projects often consume vast resources and are not in the company's strategic portfolio.

➤ Strategy-makers at all levels should remember that they are on the same team.

➤ Businesses should analyze and fully understand the implications of the introducing new IT systems for their organizations.

➤ Major IT systems cannot be introduced in isolation from wider changes to the business; therefore, it is essential that businesses thoroughly analyze the implications of implementing a new IT system. Failure to manage change is likely to result in IT systems that do not meet business requirements or in delays in implementing key operations. It may also mean that business users are unable or unwilling to obtain the most from the system. Introducing new systems should be based on clear business requirements. Analyzing and writing a good statement of business needs requires a wide understanding of the business, its processes, the supporting information flows, and future business needs. The business requirement specification must include implementation and operational needs. It is not always possible to specify fully the requirements in advance — a well-planned project should be able to take advantage of requirements and capabilities as they are discovered, provided that they are judged relevant to the core business objectives and do not increase risks disproportionately.

## ➤ Strategy Completion Checklist

The project sponsor should ensure that the following core documentation or deliverables are filed within a main project folder in order to complete the strategic phase:

- ➤ Project prioritization schedule, which lists all priority projects
- ➤ Marketing material in support of concept
- ➤ Business and IT strategic plans
- ➤ Executive reports
- ➤ Minutes of the meeting authorizing project decision
- ➤ Any correspondence relating to the project

# Chapter 2

# Becoming an IT Project Manager

We'd all like to be like Tiger Woods or Ernie Els, but we're not, so my answer to you is to get over it. The best we can do is to hit our drive in the fairway, knock an iron shot in the middle of the green, make some putts, and keep grinding away. Who knows where the practice will take you? The same applies to project management.

I'm a huge fan of project management as a business management discipline—all its technologies, processes, techniques, skillsets, tools, and annual conferences make it one of the most exciting jobs in existence today. Call it common management sense, or whatever you like, it really is a rich and rewarding profession. Chances are you'll enjoy it and turn out to be a great project manager. However, lose the idea that being a project manager is a walk in the park. It's not. You don't simply put a manager behind some project management software that you bought from some very famous company. Lose the idea that it's an easy undertaking. It's a slog up a mountain. It is dirty, hard work, and it is absolutely necessary. By working hard at specific projects, you will eventually become more and more proficient and knowledgeable at running projects. The following section shows an analogy for the project management experience.

For centuries, mountain people of the Himalayas (called Sherpas) have navigated the extreme conditions of the Khumbu region in Tibet, near Mt. Everest. In 1953, after a dozen failed attempts, a Sherpa named Tenzing Norgay became one of two men ever to reach the summit of Mt. Everest, known in Tibet as "Goddess Mother of the World." To this day, Sherpas are enlisted for their unique knowledge of the terrain and command of the high altitude. Their experience helps climbers the world over reach the summit. Similarly, project managers are often faced with incredible barriers that seem impossible to overcome — either due to technology or project complexity — that can be bridged by using skilled mentors and experienced project managers who have navigated these knowledge areas before.

## ■ PROJECT MANAGER—TRENDS

I expected a certain, sudden expansion and flow of IT project managers to rise, tsunami-like, by the time this book was finished. No such thing. Good project managers are hard to find. However, one trend is certain: Just before one project has been successfully implemented, changes are already being made on that project and another project release is in the planning. Isn't that frustrating? There are already more projects than there are project managers and it is mind-boggling how many projects are becoming more technologically advanced and integrated than ever before. What a challenge we are all faced with today! Project managers (including both those new to the profession and existing ones) have to be able to deliver projects successfully. Sufficient to say, project management is one of the most sought after professions in the world today.

Organizations select people to manage projects based on their high levels of personal productivity and their ability to get things done. These project managers are typically task-oriented people with a strong sense of urgency and a keen focus on getting started and finishing.

All types of industries are adapting to the changes in technology and, accordingly, do not hire people with the necessary skills in project management which can deliver these new projects. The functional line managers are often not considered, as they are familiar with operational business issues and are not always suitably skilled to work across organizational boundaries. Projects today need to be managed by people not only with the knowledge of project management, but also with the right stuff!

In this chapter I illustrate and address what the "right stuff" is and the path to becoming a project manager. Clients expect project managers to be competent and be able to deliver solutions, irrespective of the complexity. At its simplest approach, project management is very basic. It is very much like any other kind of management, which covers general management practices such as planning, organizing, directing, and controlling. Project management, however, concentrates on additional disciplines, such as integration, risk, communications, time, and many other relevant aspects that are required to effectively deliver a project on schedule, cost, and quality.

A colleague once asked me if project managers were really needed, as current management was already in place. I think an answer to that would have been that even the world's best soccer team still needs a team captain to lead them.

Project management uses a common set of processes and standards, which are utilized throughout any project. The trend is that project managers have to be able to cope with

**Figure 2.1**  The elements of project management

constantly changing technologies and methodologies, which if ignored can result in a project becoming obsolete or full of changes before it is even completed.

Project managers in the IT industry today, however, are faced with having to keep pace with an ever-increasing technology that changes at a very rapid rate. These factors contribute to the importance of choosing the appropriate person leading the project. My experiences, as both consultant and practicing project manager, have led me to realize that today's project manager needs a simple, yet practical approach to managing projects (see Figure 2.1).

## ➤ Project Sponsor Responsibilities

The project sponsor, in taking on the role, accepts overall accountability to the organization for achieving the project goals. The project sponsor is, in reality, the boss. The sponsor is typically a senior person within the organization who has a high impact on the business, has the necessary experience relating to the project being undertaken, or has the organizational ability to make things happen. The sponsor could also hold the title of senior manager, director, CEO, or CIO. The sponsor sees that things get done in ways that would normally take the project manager forever and a day to complete. The sponsor also reviews the overall progress of the project and serves as the source of support if there are conflicts. The individual who assumes the role of project sponsor would be responsible for

➤ Selecting the project manager

➤ Establishing the project goals

➤ Providing leadership for the overall team

➤ Selling the project to stakeholders

➤ Resolving crucial risks and issues, if the project manager cannot resolve them

➤ Ensuring that the project manager is communicating progress and following the best approach

➤ Ensuring that approval is provided to proceed to the next project phase

➤ Approving major project changes (together with the Change Control Board (CCB))

➤ Providing overall direction for the project

➤ Potentially assisting in obtaining valuable resources when the project demands it

➤ Assisting the project manager with appraisal and performance reporting

**Table 2.1**  Typical project sponsor acceptance checklist

| Acceptance List for Project Sponsor | Yes | No | Unsure |
|---|---|---|---|
| The project is already underway and is in bad shape. | ✓ | | |
| I have the available time to dedicate myself to being a project sponsor. | ✓ | | |
| I will enforce unfavorable decisions where needed to guide the project forward. | ✓ | | |
| I will place the project on hold or cancel the project if appropriate. | | | ✓ |
| Success is possible by interfacing with the project manager/team. | ✓ | | |
| I will be able to sell the project to stakeholders where required. | ✓ | | |
| I am able to motivate and pursue the necessary resources for the project. | | ✓ | |
| **ACCEPTANCE SCORE** | 5 | 1 | 1 |

Before taking on the role of project sponsor, there are some key questions that the identified individual needs to ask him- or herself and others, as an assessment and personal commitment will be necessary. Table 2.1 identifies a brief "acceptance checklist" used on an IT project.

Based on the acceptance score of 5 in Table 2.1, the project sponsor is able to see that the majority of issues can, in fact, be agreed upon, and that the role of project sponsor is acceptable. For the two items that remain unresolved, the project sponsor must ensure that a mechanism be established that will allow these items to be performed by the sponsor or delegated representative.

# ■ IDENTIFYING THE PROJECT MANAGER

During the past few years I have often encountered project managers that are well qualified but lack the necessary skills for leading a project. Project managers have to be more than just qualified and appointed to the position of project manager. The profession not only entails familiarizing oneself with key knowledge areas and being certified, but also having the practical ability to get by on the job. Today, the art of project management covers so many fields that the project manager starts wearing many hats in a variety of disciplines: Project managers are unique and multiskilled, in that they are able to function in almost any environment. The first prerequisite is to have a solid understanding of project management. What makes a good project manager? In my personal experiences I have found that project managers with the good leadership skills who work well with people contribute hugely to a project's overall success.

I am always so fascinated when I see how other people would do under similar circumstances. During the writing of this book, I observed a colleague of mine who manages about $15 million a year in IT projects and manages up to fifty IT staff. He gained success largely due to his ability to build strong relationships with all his clients and project teams. The clients absolutely enjoyed having him around. He commanded a loyal network of repeat clients and successful projects. I estimate that out of all his projects, sixty percent came from repeat business and leads and forty percent were from loyal referrals. I was intrigued to find out what his secret was, so I redoubled my efforts on assessing the things that he did well. They include the following traits:

➤ He was enthusiastic and optimistic about all his projects.

➤ He had excellent relationships with all his client and project staff.

➤ He knew how to work with people and showed his appreciation for good work on his project.

➤ He knew what was expected from him and was dynamic in moving forward with the next series of tasks.

## ➤ Project Manager Selection and Appointment

The project sponsor should formally appoint a project manager as early as possible, before the initiation phase of the project, and not leave the project until after the it has begun. For most projects it is unlikely that the project manager will be someone who works for the company. The longer it takes to appoint a project manager to a project, the more likely the chances are of having schedule slippage problems. The reasoning is that most project managers are brought on board too late, and they require some time to become familiar with the technical and project requirements. This setback impedes the entire effort. So many projects start without any formal project process or involvement of a project manager. The reason is that these types of projects are started by either the marketing or business departments within organizations.

Appointing project managers is extremely difficult; one manager is, simply put, more productive than the others, and it is extremely difficult to tell them apart just by looking at an impressive resume. I therefore have learned that when it comes to hiring a project manager, an employer cannot take a resume too seriously. A company can only learn the value of the project manager once he or she has started the actual project, as the talents lie in the day to day project management. But when selecting project managers, an employer often does not have that kind of luxury. In lieu of personal knowledge about a project manager's skills, prospective employers should focus on the job candidate's most recent project responsibilities, techniques, and methods. Often, asking the candidate to respond to a hypothetical scene is a good way to determine the candidate's suitability as a project manager (e.g., requesting that a candidate illustrate the methods and techniques that he or she uses on a project). Additionally, good candidates would be able to market themselves better by describing the value they would bring to the organization. Some of the key factors in identifying a suitable project manager are

➤ Ensuring that the individual can sustain the role of project manager throughout the project life cycle

➤ Gaining support from other departments or managers in selecting the individual

➤ Ensuring that the individual has the appropriate skillsets and knowledge

I clearly recall a troublesome project at a Fortune 50 client, who had appointed the wrong project manager to lead the project. The immediate results were rosy, but they resulted in a project that was eighteen months behind schedule, over budget by $250,000, had ineffective documentation, and had a baseline that gave a new meaning to the word "flexible." The project was an utter failure, and the individual was merely reassigned to another department. After reviewing the project results, it was decided that success could have been achieved, had the correct project manager been assigned to the helm (see Figure 2.2).

## ■ ATTRIBUTES OF A PROJECT MANAGER

For about three years as a project manager, I failed to listen to my team members and came across as arrogant. The

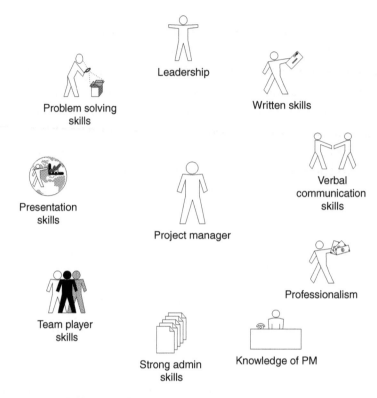

**Figure 2.2**   Skills needed by project managers

one thing I learned from experience is that right action gets right results and wrong action gets wrong results. This kept driving me compulsively to consider what attributes I needed to possess if I ever was going to be an outstanding project manager.

Project management, as a profession, has changed through the years and has produced many good project managers who have risen to higher levels, consulted world-wide, and often started their own organizations due to their broader understanding of business principles. Within the project management profession, a manager quickly becomes well-known in a very short period of time; clients identify those project managers who are good and those who cannot perform well (see Figure 2.3). The following personal attributes demonstrate the profile of a good project manager:

➤ Self-confident

➤ Problem solver

➤ Good listener

➤ Able to gain the respect of the team

➤ An effective communicator

➤ Capable of reacting dynamically and making decisions quickly

➤ Considered a professional

➤ A team player

➤ Knowledgeable about project management

Project management consultants are normally distinguishable from other company managers by the following attributes:

1. *Reputation.* The project manager is well-known by name in his or her industry and is often called upon to deliver papers, case studies, and new concepts to this audience.

2. *Experience.* The project manager has sufficient experience and has completed many projects.

3. *Leadership.* The project manager possesses the necessary leadership skills to lead people.

4. *Presentation skills.* The project manager has the ability to communicate on all levels in order to inform about project status.

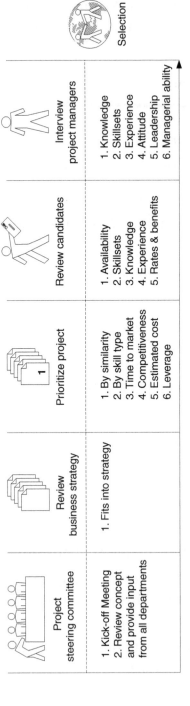

**Figure 2.3**  Understanding the need for good project candidates

5. *Expertise.* A project manager is normally employed because he or she is an expert on the subject and can speak with confidence on any project discipline.

6. *Professionalism.* The project manager, who belongs to reputable project organizations, abides by a code of ethics specifically designed for the project profession, thus ensuring that clients, organizations, and society are able to entrust project managers with their daily duties.

## ➤ Knowledge of Project Management

The first step for a newcomer to become qualified in project management is to complete a program of education. Meeting with others who are learning about project management is helpful, but it takes time. Alternatively, a prospective project manager can gather the information on his or her own. Those new to the profession don't always need degree programs or pay large sums of money just to learn project management. Many of the world's leading project managers learned their skills and techniques from experience and on-the-job training. That's where the best secrets lie, and that's why I thought sharing my experiences with project management would be helpful.

## ➤ Technical Authority

Project managers often tell me that, as project managers, they do not need to understand the technology or technical issues because the technical resources working on the project will be responsible for the technical detail. Unfortunately, in the IT environment today, it is important for all project managers to be well-versed in the relevant project technology (including its applications and processes) and be able to communicate on technical issues with the "techies." The majority of organizations that employ project managers insist that the project managers be able to take technical decisions and that they possess the necessary technical skill sets to be on a similar level as the technical staff.

I have heard many IT resources complain bitterly about project managers who haven't got the foggiest notion of what needs to be done technically. The result is often that many of these resources simply carry on with their own development process and view the project manager only as an administrative manager who coordinates time sheets and ensures the delivery of status reports.

Project managers who are not well versed on the technical level find themselves (1) isolated, (2) lacking in credibility, (3) not consulted technically on major development issues, (4) not taken seriously, and (5) possibly even provided with false information. Project managers who understand the technology and can use it practically can apply such knowledge with outstanding results. Project managers also need to be certain that they have obtained the necessary project authority from the project sponsor and then communicate this to all stakeholders. This senior executive involvement often does the trick!

I always encourage project managers to make technical decisions if and when an opportunity arises, or to be involved in any way possible, by playing the role of facilitator or negotiator with the staff.

Sun Tsu said

*If the general's employment of his mind is not in harmony with the army, even though the formation's lightness and heaviness are correct, and the front and rear are appropriate, they will still not conquer the enemy.*

## ➤ Ability to Identify and Resolve Problems

Problems will arise on any project, no matter how much planning and effort have been made to avoid them. Recovering from any such problem means that the earlier the project manager can address the problems, the better. Identifying problems may require the project manager to review tasks with resources in order to find the real causes of these problems. If the causes are not within the manager's own control or authority, then he or she must go to the project sponsor and seek advice there.

As alarming as this may seem, it may mean stopping the project until a solution is found, which is a good suggestion. Remember, the earlier you make the input to correct things, the smaller the input required. Continuing to let tasks and milestones go off track will make it more difficult to correct the situation.

## ➤ Ability to Take Decisions

An important attribute of any project manager is the ability to take decisions on a project. In meetings, project managers are often challenged to make decisions that are crucial in moving the project forward. If the project manager cannot effectively make decisions, the project surely fail.

## ➤ Ability to Select and Manage a Project Team

It is important that the project manager be able to draw up a preliminary list of people who will be needed on the project. He or she can be do this by selecting those individuals who are available within the organization and who possess the relevant skills and experience required by the project. The project manager should be able to guide and initiate the external hiring process for those team members who are

**Table 2.2**   Team selection checklist

| Selection Criteria | Necessary |
| --- | :---: |
| Candidates have the skills and expertise for the project. | ✓ |
| Candidates are available to remain for the full duration required on the project. | ✓ |
| Candidates are team players. | ✓ |
| Candidates are results-orientated and can set goals. | ✓ |
| Candidates are optimistic about the project and outcome. | ✓ |
| Candidates are trustworthy. | ✓ |
| Candidates are able to work on multiple tasks in isolation. | ✓ |

unavailable. Table 2.2 lists some of the key factors that should be kept in mind when selecting team members.

Remember, once the project manager has selected the team members, the success of the project will depend on the manager's ability to keep the team focused, optimistic, and committed to achieving the overall project objectives. However, it is not uncommon for personal problems to arise while working on a project, and the project manager should be able to identify many of the symptoms ahead of time. The project manager should have the experience and ability to work with all people, irrespective of any individual's race, religion, nationality, age, or gender. The project manager and the individual should immediately deal with any conflict that arises, and the manager should use the most appropriate course of action to resolve the problem. Additionally, the ability to praise and recognize the project team is important. It is essential that when the team has worked hard to meet objectives, often under difficult circumstances, that they are awarded the recognition.

## ➤ Having a Professional Approach

Project managers should want to be considered as professionals. The status affects the quality of life for all people on the project, organization, and even in society. Therefore, it becomes vital that a project manager conducts work in a professional manner in order to earn and maintain the confidence of team members, colleagues, employees, employers, clients, and the public. The following is a code of ethics that project managers should use to help maintain their professionalism:

➤ As project manager, I will strive to maintain high professional standards in the preparation and delivery of my projects, and I will be held accountable for the success or failure of those projects.

➤ Regarding the actual work aspect of my project, I will strive to provide the leadership, trust, tools, and support to ensure all projects are completed on time, within cost, specification, and to my clients' requirements.

Professionalism refers to being able to encourage respect and honesty in all business-related matters and during the course of any project. It is important that project managers ensure that all client or employer information be kept confidential and not lead to a situation where there is a conflict of interest.

Project managers also have a duty to their respective communities, by ensuring that no project be implemented in any location where it could possibly place lives and property at risk. An appropriate quotation from one of history's famous project managers can be used to describe ethics.

*The general must be righteous. If he is not righteous, then he will not be severe. If he is not severe, then he will not be awesome. If he is not awesome, then the troops will not die for him. Thus righteousness is the head of the army. —Sun Tzu*

### ➤ Project Management Consultants

Being hired as a project management consultant presents a unique set of challenges. First, as a consultant, the project manager has been employed by a client because that manager possesses or has demonstrated the necessary ability to manage projects. Second, this project manager also has to adjust to the client organization and people, and this can take time to ramp up. The following are some of the issues that a project manager can expect to find and adjust to at a client site.

*Challenges*

> ➤ Adjusting to the prescribed client project methodology or processes

> ➤ Obtaining an understanding of the organization and its functional areas

> ➤ Understanding organizational politics (e.g., who controls the project)

*Benefits*

> ➤ Having an objective platform to consult on project processes, techniques, and methods without any career limiting moves

> ➤ Being able, as an independent consultant, to ask the questions other permanent staff usually must avoid addressing

### ➤ Managing Virtual Project Teams

For many project managers, managing a virtual project team is becoming an ever-increasing reality, as more and more organizations are integrated and drawn together on a global scale. Geographically dispersed team project teams are common in the new global economy. I recall being assigned to manage a project in New Jersey, where I quickly found out the locations of my project team:

➤ The contractor was located in Georgia.

➤ The executive sponsor was located in California.

➤ The business owners were located in New Jersey.

➤ The developers were respectively located in Germany, Ireland, and Singapore.

➤ The analysts worked mostly from their homes in Virginia, New York, and Pennsylvania.

Today, project teams establish communication primarily through the use of electronic meeting rooms. Communication tools such as telephonic conference bridges, e-mail, calendars, document sharing, and video conferencing are becoming more common on project meetings. The biggest challenges encountered on virtual projects are taking international time zones into account, understanding one another, and establishing a platform for effective communications (see Figure 2.4).

The project manager relies on the integrity of the virtual project team to receive and understand their respective delegated project tasks and perform them accordingly, without these resources coming back and stating they did not understand the urgency and full nature of the task. In order to help the success of the virtual team, the project manager needs to establish certain criteria.

➤ The project manager should be certain that effective electronic communication tools are put in place. (i.e., e-mail, Internet, Voicemail, etc.) Any e-mail system

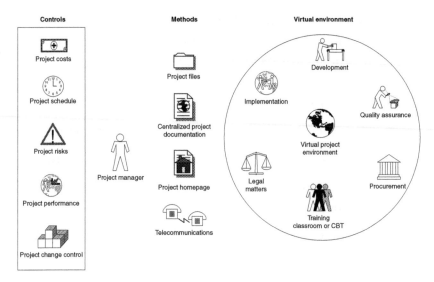

**Figure 2.4**   Working with decentralized teams and projects

should be setup correctly, in a standardized manner, in order for all members to receive and send mail.

➤ Mail should be written in an effective manner that communicates the precise information to the recipients.

➤ The project manager should develop and implement a communication plan that guides virtual project members on all the communication formats used on the project, frequency of meetings, time zones, mail, how to deal with urgent tasks, and so forth.

➤ The project manager should set up a centralized project information portal for all virtual members to access the relevant project data and information.

➤ He or she should create a schedule of pre-arranged telephonic conference calls for project status meetings.

Table 2.3  IT project manager responsibilities

| Responsibilities | Checklist |
| --- | :---: |
| Define and scope the project correctly. | ✓ |
| Identify and select project resources—team and material resources. | ✓ |
| Lead the project team through each phase of the project. | ✓ |
| Estimate and create the project budget. | ✓ |
| Identify and manage all issues and risks on the project. | ✓ |
| Create and maintain the project plan. | ✓ |
| Manage all changes to the project. | ✓ |
| Ensure that all project tasks and deliverables remain on track and within cost. | ✓ |
| Identify organizational politics and play it well. | ✓ |
| Manage the project folder and related documentation. | ✓ |
| Communicate and maintain project progress on meetings and status reports. | ✓ |

> ➤ He or she should arrange a face-to-face meeting during project initiation at a kick-off meeting or workshop, a face-to-face during project execution, and another one after project implementation.

### ➤ Project Manager Responsibilities

The role of the project manager is so critical on a project that it is important to identify the minimum basic responsibilities that are required from project managers. Table 2.3 lists these responsibilities.

## ■ LEADERSHIP ON THE PROJECT

The main difference between a leader and a manager is that leaders have followers! Project managers need to identify what leadership potential they possess. The following section presents some of the most frequently used types of leadership style I have encountered.

### ➤ Charismatic or Referent Power

These project managers, through shear personality and their position held within the company, have the ability to quickly motivate and influence project team members. Naturally, the force of the manager's personality commands the attention of the project staff: They tend to listen and to do the manager's bidding.

### ➤ Judicial or Formal Power

Project managers who fall into this category are normally respected, confident, friendly, and have a sense of purpose to see the project through to the end. They are also empathetic to the project staff. Many project managers fall within this category.

### ➤ Situational Power

This style is often a combination of leadership styles and is dependent upon the specific situation that demands it. Project managers in this category may exhibit an autocratic style in one situation and a more judicial style in the next. For example, on Monday, a subordinate on a project authorizes project changes from a vendor without the project manager's knowledge, resulting in the project manager reprimanding the member for the wrongful action. On Thursday, however, this same project manager gives the project team a motivational speech, complimenting them for all their hard work.

# ■ THE PROJECT MANAGER OF TOMORROW

Today's trends indicate that the majority of employment agencies and employers are establishing tough entry criteria for any prospective project managers. Clients have learned from past experiences that a project manager at the helm of an important project does not necessarily imply success. Instead, clients are setting higher standards for future project incumbents. Clients expect project managers to be able to

➤ Run projects autonomously and manage themselves

➤ Accurately estimate and track project schedules and costs

➤ Communicate quickly and efficiently at all levels of business

➤ Be creative and think out-of-the-box

➤ Understand how businesses work, who runs them, and what it costs to run them

➤ Be accountable for a project's success

➤ Ride the wave of change and be able to integrate the products into the market

# ■ LESSONS LEARNED FOR BECOMING AN IT PROJECT MANAGER

Without learning from past mistakes or experiences, a project manager will never be able to succeed. Several lessons I have learned from include the following:

➤ It is important to understand the technical aspects of a project and attempt to make technical decisions;

otherwise, the project team will lose confidence in the project manager's ability and may start to make their own decisions or even ask other managers for their opinions.

➤ A project manager should never continue on a project where there are two project managers running the same project.

➤ There must be a project sponsor in place or the project will not have the backing to push it forward.

## ➤ Phase Completion Checklist

The project manager should ensure that the following contractual documentation and items are obtained from and negotiated with the client prior to starting the project:

➤ Letter of appointment as project manager

➤ Verification of project sponsor identification and selection

➤ List of duties and responsibilities

➤ Written agreement of an incentive program (if both project and organizational goals are met)

➤ All completed administrative forms, such as security clearances and access

# Chapter 3

# Project Concepts

## ■ PROJECTS IN MOTION

This chapter explains the core fundamentals of what constitutes a really good project. In addition, this chapter attempts to explain why projects seem to fail. Do projects fail because of poor estimation or because of poor implementation by the project team? Once project managers understand the basic issues involved in project management, they will more fully appreciate this chapter, which deals with project initiation.

Let me begin this chapter by stating that projects understandably (1) are temporary by nature (in that they have a beginning and an end), (2) are very unique, (3) have goals that need to be met, (4) have multiple activities that need to be coordinated, sometimes across functional departments, and (5) have high impacts to a business.

Globally, companies invest billions of dollars annually on IT solutions. In addition, many organizations offer visionary solutions that all call for knowledgeable project managers to plan, execute, control, and end projects ahead of any competition. Sadly, many of these projects come in behind schedule and over budget, and fail. Part of this book focuses on those projects in turmoil and offers ways to get the greater majority of these projects back on schedule, both within budget and within specification. Many projects are canceled before they are ever completed and many exceed their original estimates. The financial costs of these failures and overruns are just the tip of the iceberg. This chapter identifies causes of and offers ways to resolve many of these issues.

On the success side, roughly 16.2 percent of projects are completed on time and on budget. In the larger organizations, the news is even worse: Approximately 9 percent of their projects come in on time and on budget. And, even when these projects are completed, they are no more than a mere shadow of the original functional requirements.*

Today, when project managers take on a project, they must face the reality that many clients are increasingly aware of how projects must align with business processes and strategy. As a result, these clients expect project managers to be able to translate their requirements into effective implementations. Table 3.1 portrays the transition that project managers are expected to make happen.

# ■ PROJECT METHODOLOGIES

## ➤ The System Development Life Cycle (SDLC) Concept

Many organizations have their own unique project methodologies concentrating on software development and delivery. The SDLC is basically a formal set of activities and phases used to guide those involved in the project through the complete development of an IT solution. Both adopting and consistently implementing a common SDLC across an organization are vital elements in providing project man-

---

*Information used with permission of the Standish Group International, CHAOS Research Report, 1995

**Table 3.1**   Transition of client expectations in project management

| From | → | To |
|---|---|---|
| Information Age | | Knowledge Age |
| Long cycle times | | Short cycle times |
| National | | Global |
| Individual project team | | Team-based |
| Lip service | | Customer relationships |
| Cost focus | | Cost and growth Focus |
| Minimal change | | Rapid change |
| Minimal integration | | Total business integration |
| Quality | | CMM Levels 4–5 |
| Project-based | | Solution-based |

agers with the ability to deliver quality solutions for clients. One of the most popular methodologies being used today is the Waterfall methodology. It is step-by-step, linear methodology that guides a project manager to complete one phase of the project before moving onto the next. Another popular methodology is the Timeboxing methodology. It's used in situations where short, rapid development and delivery are needed (i.e., prototyping), thus allowing each phase of the methodology to be repeated until the desired functionality of the product is obtained. Each methodology has its own unique set of advantages and disadvantages, as shown in Table 3.2.

When developing any IT system it is imperative to use a phased approach in developing either a product or solution for the client. If a project manager simply went about blindly developing a software product or solution without a physical or logical structure, it is more than likely that he or she would experience tremendous frustration during the development process. The most likely problems encountered would occur in the areas of (1) communication, (2) scheduling, (3) integration, and a (4) delay on delivery targets.

**Table 3.2** Comparison of waterfall and timeboxing project methodologies

| Waterfall | Timeboxing |
|---|---|
| Advantages | Advantages |
| Most commonly used | Focuses team on immediate results |
| Sequential step-by-step process | Rapid delivery |
| | May lead to good productivity |
| Client involved early in process | Client able to see results up front |
| Disadvantages | Disadvantages |
| Not all requirements are defined up front | Requires planning for final release |
| | More complex than Waterfall process |
| Client usually sees results downstream | Need to focus on the critical path |

Primarily then, the process of system development is often modeled as a series of different phases (1 – n) that define the project life cycle. Some activities simply cannot happen, or it would be less productive for them to happen, until the preceding one has been accomplished. For example, "Approving the Technical Design Specification" needs to follow "Developing the Technical Design Specification," while "Creating the Implementation Plan" naturally follows an "Approved Project Plan." Having said this, the project manager will need to determine whether the project, or the circumstances facing it, demands variations in some of the sequencing, or parallel running of others. Table 3.3 portrays the generic, defined project phases that can be used on a project.

► **Understanding the Project Life Cycle**

Very often, team members will only be used on certain phases of the SDLC, whereas staff members who look at the quality assurance or configuration management of the proj-

Table 3.3  Various project methodology approaches

| Approach #1 | Approach # 2 |
| --- | --- |
| Concept or identification | Requirements definition |
| Analysis and design | Requirements analysis |
| Construction, building, or execution | Preliminary design |
| Testing | Detailed design |
| Quality system assurance | Implementation |
| Implementation or delivery | System testing |
| Maintenance or support | Acceptance testing |
| | Maintenance and operation |

ect will be involved throughout the project. Therefore, we see clearly that a project cannot be completed in isolation or as an individual effort. Team dynamics are a crucial consideration when selecting each team member, and each contributes his or her talents to the overall success of the project.

Most organizations can maximize improvements in their project performance by simply doing the basics right. It is not usually necessary to implement a sophisticated project methodology. In fact, if a project manager is being advised or is considering implementing some form of methodology that he or she does not fully understand, typically one of two things happen: Either the proposed approach is too complex, or the organization is not culturally ready to implement it.

## ➤ Life Cycle Phases

A successful project management process relies on two activities: proper planning first, and then project execution. These two sequential activities form the basis of every project life cycle and can be expanded to suit the control requirements of every type of project in every area of project management application. The project life cycle, characterized by a series of "milestones," determines when the project starts, the "control gates" through which it must pass, and when the project is finished. The phased life cycle approach gives businesses more time to understand and assess future requirements and to make changes during the actual implementation phase. In addition, a phased approach gives the client quick wins, even at the very first phase.

The life cycle phases are important reference points for the project manager. They identify the system development life cycle in sequential time periods that sometimes overlap one another. However, the *activities* characteristic of one phase may be performed in other phases. For example, although most of the staff effort in analyzing requirements occurs during the requirements analysis phase, some of that activity continues at lower levels in later phases.

### Discovery Phase

In the discovery phase, the project team, which usually includes the project manager and selected business stakeholders (i.e., executives, strategists, analysts), explores a client's future and assists in developing the vision and strategy the client should take. The team also transforms these actions into a workable solution blueprint that is unique for the business and IT needs of the client. Additionally, the discovery phase is an important step because it allows the team to take a snapshot of the client's current organization and its processes. This allows the project team to identify and recommend improvements (both applications and enabling technologies) needed to realize the client's vision.

### Concept Phase

In the concept phase, a requirement definition team identifies and develops the functional, technical, data, capacity, architecture, performance, and training requirements together with the client. The team pinpoints any custom functionality that may be necessary and documents this formally. The conclusion of this phase is marked by a project review, at which time the solution is presented and evaluated.

### Design Phase

The baseline functional specifications form a contract between the requirement definition team and the software development team. They also provide the starting point for preliminary design.

### Execution Phase

In this phase the development team fully designs the solution, either as separate applications, modules, or needed interfaces. Resources are allocated to assist the development team, and the team works against set timelines. Higher-level executives usually hold a set of reviews, which provides an opportunity to evaluate the design presented by the development team.

### QA Phase

The quality assurance team performs extensive testing and validation on the solution developed by the build team. Tests are carried out in accordance to the design criteria, and reviews lead to successful release of the solution, allowing the solution to be implemented.

### Implementation Phase

After the client has accepted the solution, the next step is to consider the implementation at the client organization. The implementation of the solution carries numerous responsibilities and activities, such as training of resources, client knowledge transfer, and documentation, all of which need to be scheduled and coordinated.

### *Closure Phase*

At the closure phase the several priorities need to be suitably addressed: All resources should be reassigned back to the organization, post-project reviews need to be held with the client, and sufficient post-project maintenance and support should be in place for the success of the solution.

The success of a project depends on choosing a good project management methodology at the beginning (see Figure 3.1). Three elements help ensure a project's success:

➤ Managing the project through its life cycle

➤ Monitoring and controlling the schedule, budget, quality, and risk

➤ Integrating methods and tools, which builds a foundation for continuous improvements in productivity, teamwork, and communication beyond the initial implementation

Figure 3.2 shows an example of a life cycle methodology.

## ■ FACTORS AFFECTING PROJECTS

The three major factors indicating a project will succeed are (1) timely user involvement, (2) executive management support, and (3) a clear user requirement statement. There are other success criteria, but with these three elements in place, the chances of success are much greater. Without them, organizations run a high risk of failure.

Organizations should carefully consider whether projects are too excessive to undertake in one go, as this approach may impact the success or failure of a project. This is particularly important if a project is influenced by many

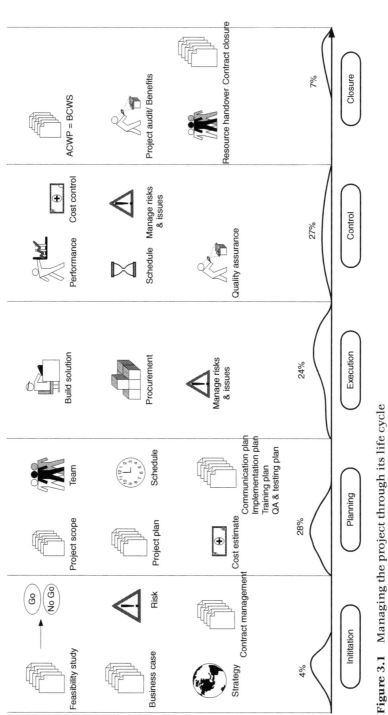

**Figure 3.1** Managing the project through its life cycle

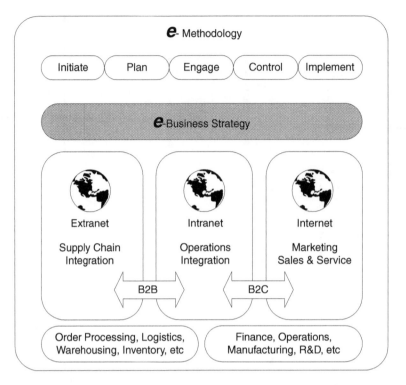

**Figure 3.2** An example of a typical e-commerce project methodology

business dependencies. The number of project failures could be dramatically reduced by dividing the entire project into relatively smaller projects or phases, with each successive one being reviewed and approved before the next one is started. The advantage of such a structured approach is that it helps to reduce the complexity of planning, monitoring, and control. Table 3.4 portrays negative factors and solutions that have been used to overcome them, thus aiding the successful delivery of projects.

The most significant cause of failure to deliver the business benefits is inadequate staff preparation and training. There are several major questions that project managers should ask when managing and monitoring a project.

**Table 3.4**   Factors affecting project management

| Factors effecting IT Projects | Recommended Solutions |
| --- | --- |
| 1. Incomplete requirements | Obtain all requirements |
| 2. Lack of user involvement | Involve all stakeholders |
| 3. Lack of resources | Develop resource planning |
| 4. Unrealistic expectations | Negotiate with the client |
| 5. Lack of executive support | Communicate with and involve executives |
| 6. Changing requirements & specifications | Adopt change control |
| 7. Lack of planning | Increase planning into the project |
| 8. Client no longer needs project | Determine requirements |
| 9. Lack of IT management | Hire correct resources |
| 10. Technological illiteracy | Train staff |

➤ Is the project's planning time scale adequate for negotiation, purchase, development, installation, training, and support?

➤ Is this still a solution that is based on a standard package implementation?

➤ Are the changes to working practices and financial procedures still minimal and controllable?

➤ Are the contract and supplier relationships aligned to the project?

➤ Does the vendor continue to demonstrate a good understanding of the business requirements?

➤ Are the mechanisms in place to manage requests for changes while the project is in progress and to identify requirements for the next upgrade to the system?

The use of appropriately skilled staff and experienced suppliers is important, and the project manager needs to be sure that he or she has obtained the best resources and made the best estimates. If the project manager selects incorrect resources, a significant increase in risk, including stopping the project, now exists.

## ■ INTEGRATION CONSIDERATIONS

Do not underestimate the time and effort needed to integrate a new system into the existing business and interface it to existing systems. Project managers need to be sure that the plan allows some contingency for slippage and that they are informed whenever staff encounters this. Project managers must plan for any integration tasks from the start of the overall project, not leave them until the end. The following are some considerations:

➤ Review those interfaces used on other projects that may influence this project.

➤ Define all project interface requirements.

➤ Be certain that there are not too many third-party contractors all working on separate integration plans. A single, coordinated effort is more desirable.

➤ Identify all possible risks and issues in a risk management plan.

➤ Define the communication between all interested parties.

➤ Define the output for each project deliverables.

➤ Document the data conversion process.

➤ Establish a change control procedure.

➤ Be certain that there is a plan for integration testing.

➤ Ensure that a contingency plan takes effect in the event of system failure.

# ■ MANAGING PROJECT RISK

Conducting a project review during a project provides an opportunity to revisit the issues and risks that the project is facing. Management and the IT project team must manage risk throughout the entire project life cycle. Using strategies to reduce risk increases the likelihood of a successful implementation.

Interviews with management project staff and key users should contribute to a frank and open discussion with a cross section of the organization's staff about the issues and risks. A key outcome of the discussions is an assessment of the overall risk that the organization needs to manage. Bringing issues forward can also help the project team highlight needed actions while there is time for proactive adjustments.

Information technology project failures make the headlines every day. With growing financial pressures and the need for successful deployment of information technology, management is increasingly focusing on the results of their investments. The project review can be an effective mechanism for senior management to ensure their projects are "under control" and are still able to deliver results.

## ➤ Identifying Sources of Risk

Internal and external risks such as poor estimates, design errors, and poorly defined roles on the project need to be identified by the project manager and the project team. Figure 3.3 shows the basic process of how to identify and manage risks.

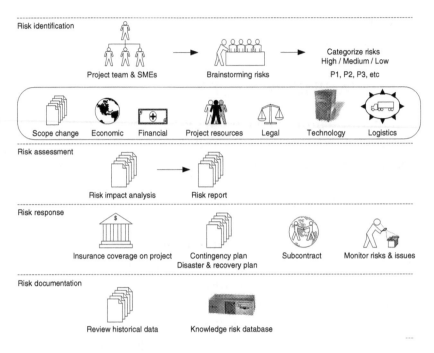

**Figure 3.3** Understanding project risk management

## ➤ Identifying Potential Risk Events

These are events that may occur during the course of the project, such as a natural disaster or a vital member of the team resigning.

Developing a risk management plan begins with a risk assessment to determine what risks exist, the potential sources of risks, their probability of occurring, and the impact on the project. Risk assessment is used to develop the risk avoidance plan, which determines the actions that will be taken to avoid risks, and the risk contingency plan, which determines the alternative actions that will be taken if the risk impacts occur. Risk assessment also defines an owner for each risk.

*Risk Analysis*

Risk analysis consists of nothing more than evaluating possible risks for the probability of them occurring, describing the potential impact, and estimating the severity of that impact. For each risk, the project manager should assign a probability ranking of *avoidable, manageable, unavoidable,* or *unknown,* along with the identification of the first possible impact date.

The risk analysis should describe the risk impact, or what will happen if the event does occur. Both tangible results (e.g., financial impacts) and intangible losses (e.g., reduced client satisfaction or team morale) should be considered in the description of the impact. This information may then be used to define impact severity.

➤ A rating of *low severity* means "workarounds" are available.

➤ A rating of *medium severity* indicates no workarounds are available; however, the risk item does not impact milestones or project targets.

➤ A rating of *high severity* indicates that risks that do not have workarounds and will impact the project milestones, target, or success.

The risks should be prioritized, for further analysis and development, based on their probability, impact date, and severity. Table 3.5 shows the various risk avoidance techniques that can be used on a project.

*Risk Identification*

For the project manager, risks can come from many sources, but they can usually be categorized into several areas.

**Table 3.5**  Risk avoidance techniques and methods

| Risk Avoidance Techniques  ⟶ | Method |
| --- | --- |
| Creating "worst case scenarios" | Hold project review with team |
| Interviews | Hold individual meetings |
| Risk questionnaire | Develop and distribute risk questionnaire |
| Decision tree analysis | Use software tool or perform manual analysis |
| Risk log | Create and itemize all known risks |

1. *Technical risks.* These risks to the project are technical in nature and are the result of complexity, integration issues, or technology. For this class of risk, project managers need to be certain that they have the required skills to deal with or mitigate any potential problems that may arise.

2. *Financial risks.* These risks include threats to the project budget—the danger of unforeseen events causing costs overruns.

3. *Schedule risks.* Schedule risks are factors that could cause delays in the project, potentially delaying the planned finish date. Often there is a relationship between financial and schedule risks in that delays often incur financial penalties and risks of delay can usually be removed—but at a financial cost.

4. *Internal risks.* Sometimes called *project risks,* these risks emanate from within the project itself. They include factors such as technical failures, delays in carrying out scheduled work, errors by project staff, and so on. Generally speaking, these are risks that the project manager can control and is in a position to do something about.

5. *External risks.* External risks, on the other hand, are threats to the project that come from the external environment. They are sometimes referred to as *business risks* and are outside the control of the project manager. Examples include legislative changes (which could render the project's products obsolete) or changing market conditions (which could render the business case invalid).

### Risk Reporting

Risks should be reported constantly throughout the project, and a process should be established whereby all risks are reported to the necessary levels within the client or company. Periodic risk meetings should also be set up with the project team and client as early in the project as possible. The top priority risks should be reported in the weekly status reports along with the current status of completion.

### Risk Mitigation

Mitigation is the process of creating strategies to minimize the impact of the risks on a project. Mitigation strategies should determine the highest risk and its associated priorities first. It is possible that, for lower types of risks, the strategy would be to take no action and prepare contingency plans in the event that they should ever occur. The processes for developing mitigation strategies are as follows:

➤ Define the approach or steps to take.

➤ Identify contingency plans for a worst case scenario.

➤ Assign responsible parties.

➤ Define the closure date and necessary criteria.

# ■ PROCUREMENT ON THE PROJECT

## ➤ Responsibility for Procurement on the Project

The project manager is responsible for ensuring that the necessary steps have been taken to procure items for the project phases, and that this process has taken into account the various lead times for delivery to the implementation site.

Under normal circumstances the project manager has a procurement manager or assistant working within a corporation or company who does the ordering and administers the purchase ordering and receipt of project goods. However, the project manager should be sure that the assistant understands the procurement process and that he or she is aware of delays caused by administration, payments to suppliers, and invoicing details. The project manager should be aware of any legal implications when placing contracts and purchasing equipment or services from suppliers and contractors.

## ➤ Procuring Products and Services for a Project

The project manager should identify from the project Work Breakdown Structure (WBS) which tasks require (1) hardware, (2) software, or (3) those services or materials related to the project. Accordingly, once identified, the project manager documents these required IT items into a standardized specification. This specification is accordingly distributed to more than one supplier for quotation.

Once the project manager has received all the necessary quotations, the process of evaluating and selecting the best products or services and of selecting a preferred supplier begins. The best price is not always the most important factor for supplier selection, and project managers should assess third party suppliers by means of developing a criteria suited to the IT solution. Table 3.6 displays a minimum set

**Table 3.6** Vendor selection criteria

| Selection Criteria | Supplier A → | Supplier B | Supplier C | Supplier D | Supplier E |
|---|---|---|---|---|---|
| Experience | ✗ | ✓ | ✓ | ✓ | ✗ |
| Cost | $125,000 | $100,000 | $80,000 | $167,500 | $94,000 |
| Compatible technology | ✗ | ✓ | ✗ | ✓ | ✓ |
| Certified staff | ✓ | ✓ | ✓ | ✓ | ✓ |
| Project management | ✓ | ✓ | ✓ | ✓ | ✓ |
| Support (24x7x365) | ✓ | ✓ | ✗ | ✗ | ✓ |
| References (x 3) | ✗ | ✓ | ✓ | ✓ | ✓ |
| Geographic location | ✗ | ✓ | ✓ | ✓ | ✗ |
| Providing of documentation | ✗ | ✗ | ✗ | ✓ | ✗ |
| Training | ✓ | ✗ | ✗ | ✓ | ✓ |

of vendor selection criteria that is used to determine which vendor is best qualified to meet the project objectives.

## ■ THE PROJECT OFFICE ROLE

The project office is often referred to as a "center of excellence" or "project support office." In basic terms, as organizations grow their project portfolios, they need to centralize all project information in order to reflect the best interests of the company. The project office should consist of both project managers and project administration staff. Project offices exist at different levels within a company, and it is not uncommon to find more than one project office within the larger organization or in different functional departments. An example of this is an IT project office that looks after the IT investments and projects within a large company, and, within that same company, an executive-level project office that reviews all projects throughout the company.

I don't think it's a necessity to have project managers running a project office, but they definitely should have input into its development and should be accountable for their projects. A project manager brings a wealth of valuable information regarding standard project management practices as defined by the Project Management Institute (PMI), as well information about as the development, direction, and adherence to a particular organization's methodologies. That is not to say that admin staff cannot perform the role of running the project office, but they should be skilled in all facets of project management to ensure its success, and they should adhere to the guidelines set forth by the company's project management professionals.

## ➤ Roles and Responsibilities of the Project Office

A project office should report on any project-related information that is crucial to the success of delivering solutions and projects within schedule and budget and should not place the company at risk. The needs of specific project office roles differ among organizations, but they all share some common distinguishing responsibilities (see Figure 3.4). Project managers should remember that it is up to the company to determine the type of data it needs in order to deliver valuable information. Typical examples of what a project office is responsible for are

- ➤ The communication of project status

- ➤ Categorization of projects (by manager, status, priority, department, region, etc.)

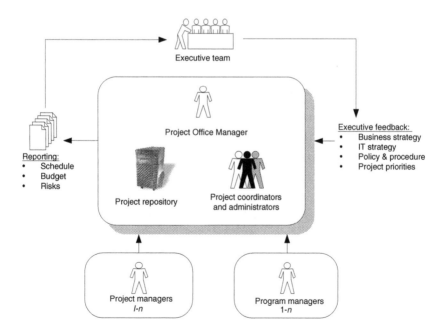

**Figure 3.4**  The project office dependency

➤ Resource allocation (by project and across multiple projects)

➤ Issues tracking and resolution

➤ Defect tracking and resolution

➤ Document repository for project-related documents (i.e., scope docs, technical requirements, project charter, agendas, meeting minutes, contracts, project matrix, change management decisions, etc.)

➤ Time tracking of tasks

➤ Integrated cost and schedule status

Many project offices should develop or use an application that allows organizations to update and report on the latest project information. Because this information is contained in a database, the information can be reported using a common reporting package or by exporting to a common format that could then be pulled into a spreadsheet for additional analysis.

An effective project office will recognize the need for different levels within the company to be supported by such a system. For example, for all projects within the company, executive management may want to see rolled-up information that has the ability to reveal more details if they need more specific information. Project managers may need access to the entire project information on projects for which they are responsible. And team members may only need access to certain information relating to their involvement in each project. Using login security and permissions in a flexible environment that is easily configurable for each individual workgroup can support this requirement.

My best advice to project managers would be to examine the needs of the company and determine the requirements of a project office that will support business processes, goals, and vision. Then, research available solutions to support these requirements or determine if it is feasible to build a customized system in-house. Obtain recommendations from other organizations (both in and out of the industry), or even take a test drive of the commercial applications available. Some areas a project office should be responsible for include

➤ Business case development

➤ Project plans (development and maintenance)

➤ Facilitation of status meetings

➤ Risk management

➤ Issue management

➤ Communication planning

➤ Documentation standards

➤ Budget monitoring

➤ Upper management reporting

# ■ TYPES OF PROJECTS

Most IT projects are categorized into the following areas: (1) infrastructure, which includes new or improved technologies or processes, (2) maintenance and upgrades to existing systems, (3) new product development and the introduction of new distribution channels, and (4) research and development. The majority of projects are chosen because there is a demand for a new product or because businesses require enhancements to outdated systems. This being the case, project managers will likely encounter three sizes of projects: super, medium, and small (see Figure 3.5).

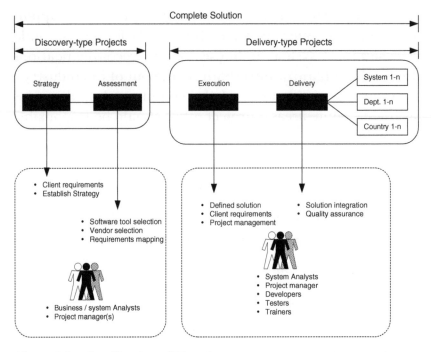

**Figure 3.5** Classification of IT projects

## ➤ Type 1: Super Projects

These projects are categorized as extremely large and complex; they often are the result of strategic decisions based on the company's strategy, architecture, and planning. Business examples of these projects include a merger of two organizations, rationalization of business processes, or the development of a new portfolio of products. In practical terms we can refer to the following examples of super projects: (1) the Human Genome project, and (2) the Mars Explorer project.

These projects often exceed eight months in duration. Super projects consume vast amounts of resources and commitment from stakeholders, and resources are assigned on a full-time basis. Normally, special controls and structures are established for these super projects. It is very common for subprojects to form from a super project, thus raising the issue of program management.

For these super projects, where a more rigid structure is desirable, organization charts are useful for clarifying roles. Each team member knows his or her role on the project, including the extent of his or her authority and responsibility.

### Early Warning Signs

The following early warning signs may indicate that a super project is going off track.

➤ The corporation is wavering in its commitment to the achievement of benefits. This may be signaled by IS advisors assuming responsibility for the project.

➤ Key project staff members have moved on.

➤ The supplier makes frequent requests for variations, clarification, or additional funds.

➤ The supplier needs redefinition of the deliverables to be supplied.

➤ There is a need to involve other parties not previously part of the project or requirements definition.

➤ There is a lack of clarity in, or frequent changes to, the organization of the supplier.

➤ There is slippage against agreed target dates for delivery of any part of the solution.

➤ There is frequent slippage of delivery dates.

➤ Project manager gets assurances that "all is well" without supporting evidence.

## ➤ Type 2: Medium Projects

These projects are categorized as being medium in size, are identifiable, and have to be architecturally aligned with the company strategy and planning. The reasoning is that these projects are dependent on other computer systems and services. Projects falling within this category follow the standard project methodology. These projects cater to the following business needs: (1) Infrastructure, (2) Portfolio, and (3) Service Delivery.

The implementation time of medium size projects often exceeds five months and is typically high profile. All the formal business analysis and project documentation is required throughout each project phase.

## ➤ Type 3: Small Projects

These are small yet important projects that need to be managed to completion. They are often encountered internally within a department or business unit. Without a project manager, these projects will surely fail, and the business operation will feel the effects. These projects often take one month or less to complete, and they do not need the formal approaches and project documentation that other projects do.

Typically, these projects would not need a business case, strategic alignment, Request for Proposal (RFP), or any contractual documentation; however, the project manager is responsible for ensuring that the project is managed according to the standard company deliverable process, in order not to lose focus. Practical examples of such small projects are (1) a server migration (2) or minor changes to a critical business application.

For smaller, more fluid projects, where it is better for each team member to work across as many roles as possible, a project manager may want to assure each individual that he or she is empowered to fill whatever roles are necessary to keep the project moving. A simple project is one where the risk to the business is low: The following list presents some guidelines to identify these projects.

➤ The solution is based on a standard implementation (usually an off-the-shelf package).

➤ The system does not cross business functions (e.g., sales and production) and does not involve a major re-design of business processes.

➤ There are no major changes required.

➤ The number of contractors to manage is only one or two.

➤ There will be no replacement of the hardware type or operating system.

➤ There are no dependencies caused by links to other projects in an IS investment program.

➤ The organization has the experience and capability to handle this type of project (i.e., it has been done be-fore, by this team, in this business).

## ➤ The Use of Project Templates

Templates are the building blocks for reusing similar forms or documents on different project phase tasks of a project. In developing any documentation or assessments for a project, the project manager should investigate using the following:

➤ Standard company templates

➤ Downloaded templates from the Internet

➤ Templates developed from the beginning

➤ Requested templates from special interest groups

# ■ PROJECT CONFIGURATION MANAGEMENT

I have found, on numerous projects, that project managers neglect to manage properly the configuration of the project (1) documentation, (2) software version, or (3) specific baseline.

Most project documents used are either in a draft stage or have not been approved by the client. Project managers share the responsibility for strictly enforcing the rule that a configuration identification process be established on the project, in order to identify all project baseline documents. The emphasis here is that only approved baseline documents with associated version control shall be used on the project. Documents should be able to be tracked based on the different version used.

The risk that is run by using unapproved project documents relates directly to the fact that the project team utilizes those documents to develop specific deliverables. The team may only find out later that the client rejected the deliverables because the client did not agree to the documents in the first place or did not review them completely. The result can be slippages in schedule and cost for the project.

Lastly, the project manager needs to insist upon and develop a method for the effective distribution and controlled releases of documentation and source code to the project team individuals or groups. The project manager normally employs a configuration manager or administrator on the project team to ensure that these necessary formal configuration reviews are executed and carried out on a regular basis throughout the project life cycle. The team members performing the configuration reviews will be able to inform the project manager or project office of the number of change requests for the project, the number of problems, and how well configuration management is being applied on the project. The project manager should identify that projects typically need the following baselines:

➤ Functional baseline

➤ Allocated baseline

➤ Design baseline

➤ Product baseline

What happens when the client decides to change a requirement after the team has started work on the project? Many projects simply accommodate those change requests into the project and the work continues, irrespective of the slippage or effects that could occur later on. The solution to this scenario is for the project manager to insist on establishing a change control process on the project for these change requests, and the full team should be made aware of how this change control process works.

The change control process must have a mechanism in place for approving, rejecting, or pending change requests. These change requests should be fully evaluated to determine their impact on the overall project before any decisions are made about the requested change. Let's assume that a change has been approved for a minor modification to the project, and it is approved without an assessment being performed. Later on, it is discovered that the training manuals and Computer Based Training (CBT) courseware were not addressed when the change was approved, and this could result in the delay of training.

Figure 3.6 reflects the flow of change requests that would occur during the project. It is important for the project manager to realize that all project change documentation is kept at the project level. Once all testing has been completed on the project, project managers obtain the necessary change

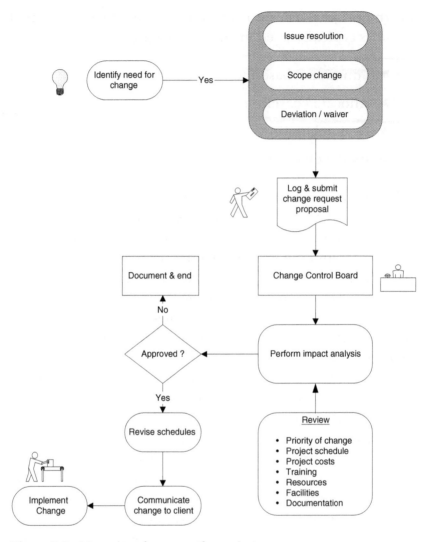

**Figure 3.6** Managing change on the project

**Table 3.7**  What project items to identify and pace under configuration control

| Project-Specific Items | Software-Specific Items |
| --- | --- |
| Project management plan | Legacy data from the client |
| Software management plan | Process specifications |
| Functional specifications | Interface specifications |
| Implementation plan | Source code and scripts |
| Operational user manuals | Database descriptions and schemas |
| Change requests | Prototypes |
| Reports | Commercial off-the-shelf software |
| Minutes of meetings | |

documentation (change requests, etc.) from the project office environment. Table 3.7 shows the configuration items to be placed under control on a project.

# ■ LESSONS LEARNED FOR PROJECT CONCEPTS

Many projects go disastrously wrong when the project management method is abandoned in order to respond to senior management pressure to speed up the project. The following are some lessons learned:

➤ The initial project definition document has no reference to the existing technology or project anymore.

➤ The project plan does not take into account the risks of integration with existing systems.

➤ Involvement of other parties was not previously identified as part of the project.

➤ Interfaces to existing systems are being raised as an issue during the last stages of the project.

*Chapter 4*

# The Project Analysis

## ■ PROJECT ANALYSIS

Most projects that fail do so largely because of ineffective analysis and poor estimation during the initial build-up phases of the project. Therefore, it is essential that the project team perform a proper analysis upstream. The rationale is that a good analysis and requirements-gathering exercise save countless hours and change requests later in other project life cycle phases. In many IT-related projects, it is crucial to identify and document exactly what the client requires prior to beginning development. Remember that good processes lead to good projects, allowing project staff to be more focused and productive. Bad processes lead to rework and inaccuracies, thus causing the project to fail.

By reading this chapter you will obtain techniques and guidelines for analyzing a project and knowing what needs to be done. This chapter provides a road map of who performs the analysis and what needs to be analyzed before launching a project. It is likely that you, the reader, may feel that analysis has nothing to do with project management at all; however, it is my opinion that analysis is very much needed, and project managers need to include the analysis or project definition phase into their project life cycle. The choice of where to start with the analysis of the project is an

important one, and it is one that needs to be carefully considered. In fact, I also believe that an in-depth understanding
of the information technology is just half of what is required
to respond to clients' needs today. The other half is a thorough understanding of the (1) client's business processes,
(2) available data, and (3) client requirements.

The Star Trek show *Voyager* provides an interesting
metaphor for the challenges of a "project analysis." During
one episode, the character Janeway, who is the captain of the
Voyager spaceship, and her crew are threatened by the re-
silient "Borg," a destructive humanoid species. Janeway in-
structs her medical and technical teams to identify and
develop a nano-virus, which will be introduced within the
Borg collective. Immediately, the Voyager crew jumps into
action, collecting data, performing various simulations and
feasibility studies, racing against time. Eventually, the ship's
holographic doctor finalizes the report makes a recommendation to Janeway. In a few short scenes, the virus is introduced into the Borg, and they are defeated! The analysis
proved to be correct.

This elegant but simple allusion shows the entire issue of
performing a project analysis: the question of whether the
project manager will be successful. So too, IT projects need
to rely on a proper analysis for any prospective concept or
idea.

The concept phase, therefore, is the stage at which the
team recognizes that a project should begin and commits
the company to doing so. During this phase, the project
team determines the project's mission, goals, objectives, and
scope in order to develop a project charter and proper feasibility documentation. This documentation is then given to
the executive team for approval, after which point, the project can commence. Table 4.1 shows which of the core business analysis tasks to complete.

Table 4.1  Issues addressed in the analysis and assessment phase

| Assess and Determine | Rationale |
| --- | --- |
| Core business processes | To assist in the business analysis |
| Information flows that support those processes | To understand the information flow |
| Interaction between processes and the functional organization | To determine interdependencies |
| What the process and data owners say they require | To establish business case |

## ➤ Project Analysis and Assessment

Executives normally require some form of business analysis to be performed on a project in order that they may obtain a summary of the benefits and implications of the intended project. The business analysis is the mechanism by which projects are approved. In the majority of cases, a project manager is tasked or appointed by executives to analyze the feasibility of the intended solution and to measure the business impact.

Depending upon the scale and complexity of the project, the project manager has to consider who will be doing the actual business analysis. There are several possible resources who could perform and execute the business analysis.

- ➤ The project manager could perform the business analysis task.

- ➤ The project manager could delegate the task to a business or systems analyst.

- ➤ The project manager could appoint external resources to perform the task.

## ➤ Analysis Tasks

The business or systems analyst identifies, researches, collects, and analyzes all required client data and information pertinent to the project. The following tasks are examples of those that are performed by the business or systems analyst:

➤ Documenting executive high-level summary

➤ Estimating value return for each dollar spent

➤ Determining the pay back period of the project, also known as the return on investment (ROI)

➤ Determining the feasibility of the project

➤ Listing all competitive threats and risks

➤ Listing regulatory requirements that could influence the project

➤ Determining the estimated number of clients the project will cover or influence

➤ Determining the anticipated growth of the client base after project implementation

➤ Determining a cost estimate for project implementation

➤ Predicting operating costs after project implementation

➤ Determining the capacity planning needed for any IT hardware or network

There is significant responsibility when assuming the role of business analyst on a project, as the entire project will base many of its finding and conclusions on the analysis that is performed. Initially, the analysts may feel excited or that they are in "emotional overdrive," as they work on defining the purpose of the project, clarify goals, meet the user community for the first time, and many more tasks.

After the brief rush of a project kicking off, many project

managers and analysts lose the ability to think "out-of-the-box," often to the detriment of both the client and the project. Clear-cut, yet creative, processes and analyses need to be established in order to complete the work. Today, it is even more critical that both project managers and analysts are creative and are able to package the analysis in such a way that it provides a forecast of future results.

Some caution is extended to analysts and project managers who fabricate results during the analysis phase due to a lack of sufficient data. The only way to provide value to any project is to be truthful, realistic, and futuristic. The outcome of the analysis clearly indicate the current client status and provide clients with recommendations with new ways to do business. Remember that a poor analysis will eventually result in the failure of a project.

## ➤ Identifying the Project Scope

The project scope is developed by the project manager and basically defines the products and deliverables to be produced during the project. The project scope takes the inputs from the user requirements and business case, and it structures the project into exactly what needs to be performed. In other words, it documents what the intended business goals are.

A common problem encountered with project scope is that the majority of initial client discussions and negotiations take place with the client and marketing executive and are carried out in isolation from the solution team. The ultimate goal of marketing executives is to market and sell solutions to clients, and when a solution is agreed upon, the client is left with the belief that it will get that specific solution. However, the technical details are left up to the solution team to resolve, and in many cases, the scope of the project changes. The project manager should work closely with the marketing manager and business analyst in order to negotiate the complete scope of work. Remember that if the scope is left untouched and uncontrolled, it is probable that your project will come in over budget and behind schedule?

It is important that the project solution team meet with the client within a few days to initiate the kick-off meeting and start defining the scope in more detail. This is where the business analysts and project manager start playing a valuable role by providing the appearance, the knowledge, and the commitment to assist the client in solving its business problems.

The project analysis team should include the client as part of the team in order to verify that the scope is defined accurately. One way to present the project scope is through the use of the project management plan or definition report. Its purpose allows stakeholders to determine quickly if a given requirement should possibly be implemented by the project. Irrespective of which document the project manager decides to use, the following should be identified:

➤ What the project scope is

➤ What the project is not

➤ How it will be managed

➤ The risks of scope change

➤ How scope changes will be integrated into the project

It is very likely that most projects will have some degree of scope change during their life cycle. Project managers should clearly understand what is included or excluded from the project, and what this effect will likely have on the entire project.

# ■ THE ANALYSIS ROLE PLAYERS

It is crucial that the roles and responsibilities of the people involved in the initiation phase be identified and that all members clearly understand what is expected from them. In the following pages, I show the types of people who are needed on a project initiation phase and what these resources are expected to deliver to the project.

## ➤ The Business Analyst

The business analyst is a necessary resource for virtually any project. In the majority of cases there are two groups of people who fully appreciate the role of the business analyst: (1) the users for whom the solution is being designed and (2) fellow business analysts. Their relationship with technical developers is confusing at times, as the two groups often battle over what actual requirements the users need and what needs to be developed. This is often a cause for miscommunication and conflict. The project manager therefore needs to facilitate this process and keep these groups focused. The tasks of the business analysts are to

➤ Listen and focus on the user requirements in order to reflect the best interest of the business

➤ Gather information and perform extensive research to support user requirements

➤ Analyze and translate user requests into well-defined documents, which the development group can use and understand. These documents could either be a (1) business case, (2) user requirement statement, or a (3) terms of reference.

➤ Develop process flows, business rules, and procedures that support the user requirements

➤ Recommend solutions that meet the needs of the business

## ➤ The Systems Analyst

Systems analysts are important resources to have on any project that involves complex, technical IT systems. They have considerable knowledge in information technology and are able to communicate both written and verbal instructions. Before deciding to employ a systems analyst, it is important that the project manager first understand what the systems analyst can contribute during an analysis phase of a project. Systems analysts perform the following roles:

➤ They assist in determining system resource requirements.

➤ They direct the work of the programmers or fellow systems analysts.

➤ They develop functional and technical analysis for large projects or systems and provide recommendations to the development manager or project manager.

➤ They review and develop flowcharts and data models from which applications will be developed, compiled, tested, and implemented.

➤ They assist in developing procedures for an application.

## ➤ The Project Manager or Project Consultant

The project manager is the leader of the project team and also contributes during the analysis phase of the project. Project managers perform the following tasks:

➤ They manage the initial project team members assigned to the analysis phase.

➤ They resolve possible conflicts and communication problems between stakeholders.

➤ They manage the project schedule and delivery of business documentation and processes.

➤ They respond to a client's needs during the analysis phase.

➤ They achieve the objectives of the business.

➤ They manage client expectations.

## ➤ The Program Manager

Unlike a project manager, who manages a single project or a few subprojects, the program manager is accountable for the coordination and integration of all project milestones and activities that are interdependent on one another. The program manager usually has strong organizational and leadership skills, and these skills help ensure that the program will achieve its intended goals. The program manager has a direct relationship with the project sponsor and individual project managers.

## ➤ The Subject Matter Expert

The project team often includes key project technical members and subject matter experts (SMEs). Subject matter experts bring expert or technical assistance to the project. Team members should be listed in the project charter to establish their roles and commitment to the project. Table 4.2 lists the technical support that a project manager should arrange to assist with the tasks of the business analysis phase.

**Table 4.2**  Technical team support during the analysis phase

| Activity | Output |
| --- | --- |
| Advise project manager on technology strategy | Offer technical advice and recommend strategy |
| Review current architecture | Review and document findings |
| Plan and motivate for technology | Offer technology support and motivations |
| Design the future technical architecture | Establish the future technical architecture |
| Build and assemble the technical solution | Build and present the feasibility of the solution |

### ➤ The End-user

The end-user usually represents the client who will be using the solution once it is implemented. The analysts therefore need to meet with the end-user on a regular basis to determine their own respective requirements. Normally, the more knowledgeable the user is, the more likely key information will be included. Furthermore, leaving the end-user out of the analysis phase can lead to last minute design changes by the development team, as important functional issues could be resolved by listening to the day-to-day workings of the user.

It is advisable that during the analysis phase of the project, the analysts obtain a list of selected end-users from the client so that the business or systems analysts may have an idea of with whom they can work. These end-users eventually will be the individuals facing the questions and will be included in necessary business meetings.

## ■ OBTAINING PROJECT REQUIREMENTS

One of the most important steps in any project is to determine accurately what the client requirements will be. It's kind of like preparing a shopping list before going out shopping. Any missing items from the shopping list will have a direct influence on the end result. Similarly, on a project, it is vital that all the necessary client requirements be defined during the analysis phase in order to move forward. The biggest risk in not obtaining and approving all the project requirements up front occurs when the client starts changing or adding additional requirements to the scope of the project. These changes obviously have an effect on pricing, resources, and schedule. So the key factor here is to ascertain exactly what needs to be done. This is why many IT projects employ the services and skills of the analyst, who is a specialist in determining these requirements.

A common mistake that project managers make is to commence work on the next phase of the project before obtaining complete or approved business requirements. Revision upon revision of user requirements may have been developed, but somehow these requirements cannot be agreed upon. Nonetheless, the project manager needs to insist upon a completed User Requirement Specification (URS) before continuing the project.

In many cases the client has not been involved during the analysis, and the end result is that the deliverable differs from the client expectations. The client, accordingly, will not sign it off until the appropriate revisions have been incorporated into the URS. This delay can take weeks, if left unmanaged, and, at this stage, the project manager should be focused on finding ways to ensure that this deliverable can be completed.

### ➤ Identifying Business Requirements

The business requirements need to be presented in a well-structured document, which forms the foundation whereby the quality assurance and testing teams accept the system.

Ideally, the outcome is that the functional requirement is a document that shows clear consistency between what is technically possible (within realistic time scales and cost) and what the business wants. However, there are a number of different scenarios that can arise.

➤ It is not possible to be sure that the requirements are technically feasible, therefore requiring prototyping.

➤ The client requirement grows to an unacceptable level of complexity, and the project conducts a review to see if the project can be split into smaller, more manageable subprojects.

➤ There is only a partial match between the requirements and what is possible, requiring a feasibility study to explore the degree of match.

Because most projects are driven by the functional specification it is vital to remember that any change in this specification automatically implies a likely change in schedule and cost. Therefore, the functional specification is to be well-documented and approved by the relevant project stakeholders. Once approved, the specification forms the baseline by which the project will develop the solution.

The project manager must understand that the cost of changing the functional specification increases substantially as the project progresses through the various phases of its life cycle. Imagine working on a project with an unsigned business requirement document and then the client informs the project that it is not what the client needed. The effect on the entire project is disastrous. Therefore, it is imperative that the client confirms and approves the business requirements.

# ■ ANALYSIS TECHNIQUES USED ON AN IT PROJECT

In the course of any IT project, it is very likely that the project manager will need to perform an analysis in order to document a solution for a client. It may be necessary that the business analysts or related project team members spend a considerable amount of time with the client identifying and gathering all the necessary information. In this situation, there are many levels of detail that need to be discussed, but the following techniques and issues must be addressed during the analysis phase:

➤ Inquiry as to whether all the data and information are available for analysis

➤ Determination of how the client currently deals with this current problem

➤ Review and documentation of the current system

➤ Inquiry as to whether appropriate time scales have been allocated for the analysis phase

➤ Presentation of alternative solutions

➤ Entity relationship diagrams

➤ Work and data flow diagrams

➤ Interviews held with users, suppliers, and competitors

➤ Personal observations

➤ Questionnaires distributed to identified target groups

➤ Research performed using the Internet, libraries, and special interest groups

➤ SWOT analysis

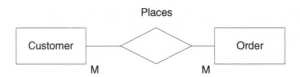

**Figure 4.1** Basic entity relationship diagram

## ➤ Entity Relationship Diagram (ERD) Technique

In the IT environment, it is at times necessary for analysts to use an entity relationship diagram (ERD) to document and model organizational information needs. Sometimes narrative descriptions cannot be used, as it can be difficult to visualize the vast amounts of data and processes in a textual format. The ERD allows the analyst to visually model the organization's information needs during the early stages of the SDLC. When constructing an entity, the project manager writes the entity's name (i.e., Customer or Employee) into rectangular boxes, which denote them as entities. Another class of object in an ERD is a relationship. Entities are also associated by relationships that represent real-world relationships (see Figure 4.1). The following are some tips for using ERDs:

> ➤ Entities are objects about which the system needs to record information.

> ➤ Relationships are recorded on the diagram as verbs and are represented by a diamond shape.

## ➤ Workflow Process Technique

Before starting any project, it is highly likely that the analyst will sketch or model some process (using media such as paper or computer). This is an important part of any IT project: Issues become very complex later on if there is no model to work from. The workflow process technique, in essence, describes how individuals complete tasks in order to achieve a result or process. It basically details how individuals communicate and interact throughout the business process, as organizations today are focusing on information and the physical interactions between the marketplace and employees. When trying to analyze an organization's current or future state, analysts must focus on this wider view.

The result of this focus is an analysis that is based around interrelated organizational processes rather than just functional hierarchies, which is a good thing. The workflow process model aims to capture this collaborative process in a visual way, representing all variables involved in its completion.

The workflow process model uses circles to represent people and squares to represent artifacts—both real and informational. Lines indicate the flow of information and all elements are labeled appropriately. Additionally, the flow lines indicating the transport medium (i.e., by hand, fax, e-mail, telephone, web, Personal Digital Assistant (PDA), etc.) are also labeled for clarity. Figure 4.2 depicts an example of a workflow process model.

## ➤ SWOT Analysis

Project managers and business analysts alike all use the SWOT technique (Strengths, Weaknesses, Opportunities, and Threats) in order to assess and become familiar with the project's overall position in the market in relation to competitors before they determine a medium- to long-term strategy. The SWOT analysis results are determined by identifying all positive and negative factors relevant to the project. The SWOT technique is usually developed in a team

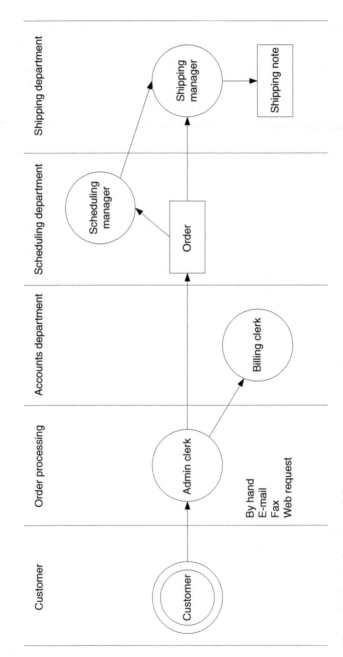

**Figure 4.2** A classic workflow process

**Table 4.3**   Internal and external analysis factors

| Internal Factors (Strengths & Weaknesses) | External Factors (Opportunities & Threats) |
|---|---|
| Clients | Economics |
| Shareholders | Regulatory and legislative guidelines |
| Competition | Technology |
| Corporate culture | Corporate politics |
| Organizational structure | Environmental elements (e.g., earthquakes, tornadoes, hurricanes) |

**STRENGTHS**
- ➤ What are our core competencies?
- ➤ How strong are we in the market?
- ➤ What do we do excel at?
- ➤ Is our strategic direction focused?
- ➤ Do we have a positive work ethic?

**OPPORTUNITIES**
- ➤ What favorable circumstances are we facing?
- ➤ Are entering new markets?
- ➤ Can we position ourselves for new opportunities?
- ➤ What is the market attractiveness?

**WEAKNESSES**
- ➤ What are our weak areas that affect the project?
- ➤ What do we do poorly?
- ➤ Do we have a plan to go forward?
- ➤ Is our organizational structure sufficient to take on the project?

**THREATS**
- ➤ What are our competitors doing?
- ➤ What are potential obstacles?
- ➤ How rapidly is technology changing our business efforts?
- ➤ What are the regulatory & legislative aspects threatening the project?
- ➤ What standards & specifications are potential threats?

**Figure 4.3**   SWOT analysis diagram

environment and all team members participate in and contribute to completing the SWOT analysis. Table 4.3 shows the factors that could deter a project from being successful.

Figure 4.3 clearly shows the format of the SWOT analysis technique.

## ➤ Life Cycle Demand Analysis (LCDA)

The business analyst should analyze and measure the anticipated usage and demands on the current information

Table 4.4  LCDA of a proposed IT solution

| Projected Life of Solution | 1999 | 2000 | 2001 | 2002 | 2003 | 2004 |
|---|---|---|---|---|---|---|
| User Demand | 1,500 | 1,875 | 2,030 | 2,300 | 2,900 | 3,200 |
| % Change | 0 | 25.0% | 8.26% | 13.30% | 26.08% | 10.34% |
| Average % | | | | | | 16.59% |

system (or systems) and what the likely demand on the new solution will be over the next few years. A technique that works well for this situation is the life cycle demand analysis (LCDA). The analyst reviews the current system by studying historical data to project back as far as possible (e.g., going back five years) and then calculating the demand for each subsequent year the system will be in use. The average can then be determined and projections made for future years. However, the analyst must carefully determine the future "volumes" or "users" that will be likely be using the system, and ensure that this LCDA is not performed in isolation.

The technique shows its value most when the results (obtained from interviews, surveys, IT administration) are displayed on a spreadsheet format for easy reference and review. Table 4.4 gives a typical LCDA for a company that would like to reflect the anticipated usage or demand of a proposed product or solution. In this example, a 16.6 percent average annual increase is anticipated. Accordingly, the analyst uses this growth factor when assessing the current and proposed utilization.

## ➤ Business Impact Analysis

It is important that the business or systems analyst evaluates which systems and functional areas will be affected by the implementation of a new solution. The analysts have to ensure that sufficient assessments have been made and that these findings are accurately documented. It would be un-

Project Title

**Business Impact Analysis**

Approval list
Distribution list
Contact persons & participants
Activities to complete this new solution
Person responsible for solution delivery
Business impact analysis
➤ Business processes affected
➤ Systems affected
➤ Environments affected
➤ Clients & users affected
Impact questionnaire
➤ List all mission critical systems
➤ Reliance on IT infrastructure
➤ Predicted risks in your area
➤ Worst case—IT failure
➤ Financial losses if affected
➤ Ability to use manual systems
➤ Available contingency plans
➤ Other
Questionnaire Consolidation & Recommendations

Doc No:                                                                    Rev 1.0

**Figure 4.4**   Business impact analysis diagram

wise to raise a red flag or mention that a crucial business department was left out of the assessment when the project has reached the physical implementation stage. Therefore, analysts need to conduct a thorough, methodical assessment to determine who may be affected and the impact this may have on the current infrastructure and resources (see Figure 4.4).

## ➤ Analyzing the Client Architecture

The business or systems analyst should analyze and document the client's current information technology architecture as part of completing the project initiation phase. Often, the business analyst faces the problem that he or she lacks the skills to perform a technical assessment of the client's architecture; in this case, the assessment needs to be delegated to an IT architect or systems analyst. The analyst should ensure that a complete inventory of the current system is documented and that this documentation includes (1) hardware, (2) software, (3) communication, and (4) the physical infrastructure. The analysis should clearly indicate whether the IT systems are (1) owned by the client or leased to independent contractor(s), (2) compatible with the current architecture and platforms, (3) becoming obsolete, or (4) suitable for the overall direction and trends of the business strategy.

There are several factors needed to perform a proper technology assessment, and these factors can be separated into three main categories.

### Hardware

Important elements to consider when addressing hardware needs include

- ➤ The Manufacturer
- ➤ Scalability of system
- ➤ Operating systems supported
- ➤ Useful / anticipated life
- ➤ Hard drive capacity
- ➤ Make of hardware
- ➤ Model
- ➤ Year
- ➤ Cost
- ➤ Memory
- ➤ Maintenance agreements

➤ Power requirements

➤ Network requirements

➤ Multimedia requirements

➤ CPU speed

### Software

Important elements to consider when addressing software needs include

➤ The manufacturer

➤ Registration

➤ Ability to be customized

➤ Licensing purchase cost

➤ Make of software

➤ Training requirements

➤ Version (e.g. Ver. 5.0)

➤ Annual licensing cost

➤ Hardware that it supports

➤ Year purchased

➤ Maintenance agreements

### Infrastructure

Important elements to consider when addressing infrastructure needs include

➤ Physical location

➤ Types of protocols (e.g., X25, ATM)

➤ Type of facility

➤ Site leased or owned

➤ Location size

➤ Equipment type

➤ Bandwidth

➤ Annual operating cost

➤ Available space

➤ Telecommunications company

➤ Power requirements

➤ Air conditioning

# ■ DEVELOPING THE BUSINESS DOCUMENTATION

During the early phase of the project, the business analysts will begin the process of documenting and formalizing all business requirements into a (1) business case, (2) user requirement statement, or (3) terms of reference document. It is vital that these documents are completed on time, and they need to be approved by all stakeholders (even the users) before being used to draw up the project documentation. The business documentation is normally co-authored or written by the project manager and managed thereafter.

The project business documentation must clearly take into account the exact client business requirements. The project manager should ensure that the documentation is consistent and does not conflict with any other requirements. The business analysis remains focused on documenting the core business benefits. It should take into account the needs and preferences of system users. Finally, the documentation should be unambiguous and should provide the reader with only one picture of what is required.

**Table 4.5** Benefits of having business documentation in place

| Documentation | Without Documentation |
| --- | --- |
| Establishes clear understanding of the project. | There is no method to reflect changes to a project. |
| Forms a baseline for documenting the project scope. | There can be legal disputes. |
| Allows for better project management in phases. | Analysis is ineffective. |
| Used for post-project reviews and audits. | Communication with client is ineffective. |
| Charts formal communication to client and others. | The result is confusion. |

Project documentation is essential to any project success. I am reminded of a time when I received an e-mail on a Friday afternoon informing me to perform a project audit on a troubled project the coming Monday morning. When I arrived on the given day and inquired about the status and whereabouts of the project documentation, I was told by the assigned project manager that there was none, as they never had any time to develop all the required documents. This statement gave me the immediate answer: Lack of documentation led to the project going off-track. Table 4.5 shows the benefits for projects that use project documentation.

## ➤ Business Case

As projects are costly exercises, it is imperative that senior executives within the organization approve spending money on the project prior to undertaking the initiative. The way in which they are made aware of the project and commit themselves to this project is through the business case. Without a formal business case, the project is likely to be cancelled within a short period of time and will have resulted in a lot of wasted effort. The business case document therefore defines and assesses the proposed project. The business analyst

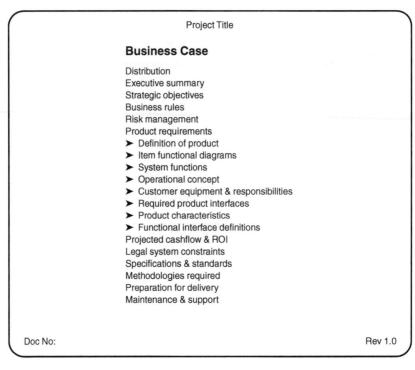

**Figure 4.5** Business case diagram

develops the business case with help from identified groups, departments, and subject matter experts, and continues to update the business case in parallel while development takes place. The business analyst and project manager, together with executive involvement, should review and refine the business case into a workable document. A copy of the business case is kept in the project file (see Figure 4.5).

## ➤ User Requirements Statement (URS)

The URS is certainly the most important document to be produced on the entire project and it is also drawn up early in the project. Of note is the fact that everyone must be aware that requirements may change. The URS therefore formally states

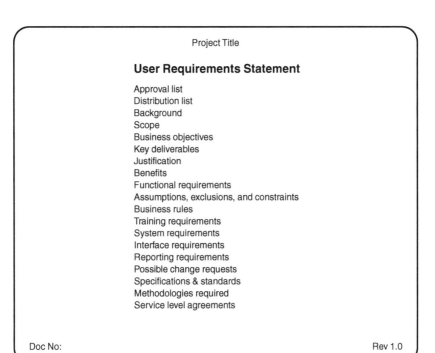

**Figure 4.6** User requirements statement diagram

the client's full business requirement after in-depth analysis of the situation. Affected end-users, IT, and management are involved from day one. It is very important to understand that the URS describes the problem and the requirement, even before any development takes place (see Figure 4.6).

## ➤ The Request for Proposal (RFP)

The RFP is written by the client and submitted to multiple contractors for their review and subsequent bidding. The bid should then be broken down into statements of work (known as SOWs) for each WBS item. I like to think of the RFP as the "what" and the SOW as the "how."

Personally, I don't like to give away too much of the "how" in a bid to the requesting client in case it is not successful. The reason is that some clients have no intention of using that particular company at all: Receiving the technical bids is a sure way of knowing how to perform the work themselves, or better still, to get another company to do it for less, based on the first company's approach. It is also customary to see some RFPs that ask for a WBS as part of the returning bid. Adjudication of competitive bids is more difficult, but it allows the client to see the different approaches to solving the problem at hand.

## ➤ Statement of Work (SOW)

The contractor bidding for the project writes the SOW and uses the RFP as a reference document. The main point of the SOW is to define the work and to divide the main deliverables and subsequent tasks into measurable items. An example of this would be describing all of the tasks that the contractor performs. The SOW explains both the management and technical approaches that will be used to meet all project deliverables. The SOW also includes key measurement and performance criteria with an emphasis on how reporting to the client will take place.

It is often the case that the client does not understand the full scope of the work to be done. However, when writing the SOW, the client expects an understandable plan that clearly states what will be delivered. The problem many SOW documents have is that they use vague language, tasks are not well-defined, and it does not clearly stipulate what the contractor is expected to do.

## ■ DETERMINING PROJECT FEASIBILITY

The project should be defined during this phase, and the definition should show that the project will be conducted in a logical and proper manner. Some of the core functions addressed during this feasibility assessment include

➤ Business purpose

➤ Benefit/cost analysis (pay back)

➤ Legal and regulatory issues

➤ Training issues

➤ Scope and detail

Executives today rely on valuable financial information to guide them in making more informed decisions about project investments. The point of assessing any potential solution for an organization is to determine if the solution will be valuable, and the analyst needs to find out ways to ensure this happens. The following are examples of reliable information that project managers can supply executives.

➤ The project ROI is 170 percent.

➤ The pay back period is 2.5 years and can be accomplished faster than anticipated.

➤ The probability of success is greater than 70 percent.

➤ The project risks have been analyzed and are deemed acceptable.

## ➤ Price Versus Cost

So very often, I encounter project managers who are not even sure about the differences between price and cost of a project. Without understanding this basic concept the project could be lost. In basic terms, price is the amount of money that a client or stakeholder is willing to give the project manager in order to receive something from him or her. As a provider, this can either in the form of a product or a service.

Cost, on the other hand, is the amount of resources (e.g., money, staff, training, materials, and equipment) that are consumed in order to produce the delivered products or services that the project has as its result. What then is the relationship between cost and price? Are we satisfied if we are able to make a reasonable profit on what we do for our stakeholders? Are we satisfied if the cost of doing a project is less, by some accepted percentage, than the selling price?

## ➤ Benefit-cost Analysis (BCA)

Organizations often regard information systems expenditure as costly and risky, and these IT investments directly affect the budgets. Despite the importance and cost, many IT investments appear to go ahead without the use of normal investment appraisal and risk management techniques. One such technique used to justify IT projects is the benefit-cost analysis (BCA). The project manager and the project team perform the BCA, as one person rarely has all the expertise to complete a BCA.

Performed during the initiation phase, the BCA essentially weighs the benefits against the costs of a project and is normally measured in monetary terms. If monetary values cannot be assigned, then relative values for benefits and costs can be used. In simplified terms the benefit-cost analysis clearly shows the project manager the "dollar burn rate." The purpose of a BCA is to support better decision–making. Project managers can use this technique to calculate for every dollar invested on the project, the dollar amount expected to receive back.

For example, let's assume that the marketing department

**Table 4.6** Calculating the benefit-cost analysis (when profit is computed in numerator)

| Assumptions | Formula Application |
|---|---|
| Estimated Benefits (Sales) = $50,000 | BC = $\dfrac{(\$50,000 \times 0.2 \times 0.7)}{\$35,000}$ |
| Probability of Success = 70% or (0.7) | |
| Estimated Profit = 20% (0.2) | = $\dfrac{\$7,000}{\$35,000}$ |
| Estimated Costs = $35,000 | |
| | BC = 0.2* |

Note: If you remove the estimated profit percentage from the benefit cost ratio formula then you calculate your break even point. (B/C ratio = 1.0). For this to happen the formula must contain revenue not profit.

*Where > 1.0: Profitable, benefits exceed the cost. Where < 1.0: Unprofitable, costs are greater than the benefits. Where = 1.0: Benefits balance cost, neither win or lose.

expects to achieve results of $50,000 on the product and the project manager has determined that it will cost the client $35,000 to implement the project. Forecasted figures show a 70 percent probability of this occurring, and estimated profits are projected at 20 percent. Table 4.6 reflects the scenario where a positive BCA is achieved.

$$\text{BCA} = \frac{\text{Estimated Benefits} \times (\text{Estimated Profit*}) \times \text{Probability of Success}}{\text{Estimated Costs}}$$

This example shows a benefit-cost ratio of 0.2. This implies that for every dollar invested, the client can expect to receive 20 cents. Which is not a bad result (20% return on investment).

Remember that when a BCA has been performed and compared to an alternative BCA and they both come out with similar costs and different benefits, then the BCA

providing the greatest benefits to the project should be selected. Accordingly, if both BCAs have similar benefits but
different costs, then the BCA with the lowest cost should be
selected.

## ➤ Calculating Net Present Value (NPV)

On any project, it is important to know what the present
value of the contract amount will be, even if the project is
scheduled over a few years. A technique available to project
managers is to discount future dollar values, or calculate the
NPV, which transforms future benefits and costs to their
"present value." The NPV allows the project manager to determine the value of a dollar one or more years from the date
of the calculation. The present value (also referred to as the
discounted value) of a future amount is calculated by using
the following NPV formula:

$$P = F \left( 1/(1+I) \right) n$$

Where P = Present Value, F = Future Value, I = Interest Rate,
and n = number of years.

## ➤ Estimating Return on Investment (ROI)

Nothing beats selling the business case better than a decent
ROI. Today more and more clients are asking what value
their IT investment dollars will bring the company. Because
they are authorizing the capital to fund a project, they would
like to know what's in it for them! Increasingly, project managers are now requested to inform their clients what their
likely returns would be because the project managers are
managing the proposed project. Project managers should
ask themselves if they would want a dollar today or a dollar
tomorrow! The following formula shows how to calculate the
ROI:

$$\text{ROI (\%)} = \frac{\text{Net Present Value of Savings}}{\text{Initial Investment}} \times 100$$

### A Project Scenario

A pharmaceutical client has assigned a project manager to replace a company's aging system with a modern e-commerce application. The executive team tasks the project manager to perform a ROI, as the project will be a large undertaking for the company. Immediately, the project manager begins to quantify several things (see Table 4.7).

The ROI of this project example is 241 percent, which means that the financial benefits exceed the initial investment by 141 percent. If the ROI were 100 percent, then the benefits would equal the cost of the project—thereby breaking even.

## ■ PROPOSING A SOLUTION

There are numerous options for recommending solutions to a client. Normally these include (1) commercial off-the-shelf solutions (COTS), (2) tailored solutions, and (3) totally new developments. Each recommendation does carry its own set of risks, and the project manager should be aware of these during the design phase. Typically, the following areas should be taken into account:

➤ The business and procurement strategies

➤ The business requirements

➤ Potential products and suppliers

The trend is a move toward greater functionality and flexibility in packaged software and a reduction in bespoke development. It is now also likely that the solution

Table 4.7  Calculating ROI

| | Yr0 | Yr1 | Yr2 | Yr3 |
|---|---|---|---|---|
| **Cost with NEW Solution** | Project* | Support | Support | Support |
| Hardware | $200,000 | | | |
| Web Software | $300,000 | $100,000 | $100,000 | $100,000 |
| Project Implementation | $550,000 | | | |
| Support | | $300,000 | $300,000 | $300,000 |
| TOTAL | **$1,050,000** | **$400,000** | **$400,000** | **$400,000** |

| | Yr0 | Yr1 | Yr2 | Yr3 |
|---|---|---|---|---|
| **Cost with CURRENT Solution** | Support | Support | Support | Support |
| Database Administrators | $600,000 | $600,000 | $600,000 | $600,000 |
| Operational Support | $800,000 | $800,000 | $800,000 | $800,000 |
| TOTAL | **$1,400,000** | **$1,400,000** | **$1,400,000** | **$1,400,000** |
| The Net Savings if Project is Chosen | ** | $1,000,000 | $1,000,000 | $1,000,000 |

**Now Calculate the Discounted Net Savings**—assuming a rate of 9%\*\*\*

Year 1: $1,000,000 \times 1/(1 + .09) = \$917,431.19$

Year 2: $1,000,000 \times 1/[(1 + .09) \times (1 + .09)] = \$841,679.99$

Year 3: $1,000,000 \times 1/[(1 + .09) \times (1 + .09) \times (1 + .09)] = \$772,183.48$

**NPV TOTAL: $2,531,294.66**

**ROI**

| | |
|---|---|
| **Discounted Net Savings at 9%** | $2,531,294.66 |
| **Initial Cost of New Solution** | $1,050,000.00 |
| **ROI** | **241%** (positive) |

\* = The comparison of the initial cost of the new solution to the cost of the current solution is not appropriate because the new solution will not be available until the end of Year 0. The comparison of the two solutions is not meaningful until the new solution is complete.

\*\* = Assumes that the project will be completed by the end of Year 0 and will be available starting Year 1.

\*\*\* = There are several options for choosing the discount rate, such as the cost of capital (e.g., borrowed from a bank), the rate of return of alternative projects, or the investment yield rate.

components will be purchased from a number of suppliers that adhere to open systems standards.

## ➤ Addressing the Solutions Capabilities

The business analyst must ensure that during the initial project meetings and design reviews, the analyst documents all the capabilities the client expects from the new solution once operational. This is an important step as most of the planning will revolve around and focus on these requirements. Typical examples of what a client should communicate to the project team include

- ➤ 97 percent system availability seven days a week (redundancy)
- ➤ Month-end reports within two days of month end
- ➤ Remote field access to 2,000 agents
- ➤ Two terabytes of disk storage space
- ➤ Help Desk agents to be able to support 50,000 inbound calls, e-mail, and faxes
- ➤ Ability to retrieve subscriber contract and accounts within twenty seconds
- ➤ Routine backup of user files and off-site storage of disaster recovery files
- ➤ Training needs

## ➤ Commercial Off-the-shelf (COTS) Solutions

In broad terms, the further the solution moves from a standard package to a tailored solution, the higher the risk in terms of cost, time, and performance, as development work is involved. The project manager should consult with the client to help the client understand that a COTS solution may be the preferred option. A COTS solution can

➤ Significantly reduce the risk of failure

➤ Deliver benefits sooner because, being done before, it can be implemented faster

➤ Cost far less than tailoring a system and redesigning from scratch

The project manager should assess each of these reasons individually against each potential business benefit, implementation cost, and risk factors. It is a good idea to hold a design review with the following project team members to evaluate and decide upon the appropriate IT solution:

➤ Development manager

➤ IT architect

➤ Systems analyst

➤ Database or systems Administrator

➤ Operations and support staff (capacity and performance planning)

If the project manager has the option of taking the packaged, standard solution approach, he or she should be aware that there are still risks that need to be managed. These risks may include having to make a long-term commitment to the supplier of the standard solution, which may constrain future IT purchasing strategy. The proprietary COTS package may be discontinued, or have insufficient functionality, which could leave the client with a problem. Therefore, the project manager and his or her technical team should always consider whether a COTS package implementation is the best selection.

## ➤ Adapting Existing Systems

An option that is frequently overlooked is that of adapting an existing system. This option may offer short-term benefits, particularly while waiting for the release of a proven version of a packaged solution, and it is a potentially low-cost, low-risk solution. However, adapting and continuing to rely on an existing system does have some risks.

> ➤ It can cause investment in potentially redundant technology platforms.

> ➤ It can create a reliance on in-house systems maintenance skills.

> ➤ It can prevent the improvement of existing business processes.

## ➤ Developing Customized Solutions

Many organizations require unique customization of available standard packaged solutions. This customization is performed in order to get the best of both worlds, but the result can be failure if the project customizes the solution too much. The key criteria here is that the client must, at some point in time, draw a line when deciding upon the amount of customization. There are two main categories that a client should consider when wanting to customize a solution: (1) limited customization and (2) extensive customization. Table 4.8 portrays the impact each of these choices have on a standard application.

The majority of software packages available on the market today (i.e., Siebel CRM, SAP, Oracle, etc.) feature some level of customization, and such projects can be implemented successfully, based upon tried and tested project methodologies. However, where the need for extensive cus-

**Table 4.8** Impact of customizing a standard package

| Limited Customization | Extensive Customization |
| --- | --- |
| Allows design of the user interface | Is likely to cause an increase in project schedule and budget |
| Offers ability to change certain documentation and reports | Causes growth in technical complexity |
| Gives definitions and changing of customized fields | Results in poor quality of functional and system fit |
| Defines customized business processes | Does not have effective support from software vendor |

tomization is identified, this becomes another matter. Extensive customization falls into a high-risk category, and the project team may need to consider other options, such as developing new software. The project team, nevertheless, needs to validate that the client requirements justify the customization as being realistic.

## ➤ Developing New Solutions

Developing an entirely new solution is always the highest risk for any client or contractor, and it should not be started without a formal assessment and completion of a (1) ROI, (2) BCA, and a (3) risk analysis. Depending upon the complexity of the solution, it may be appropriate to seek risk-sharing with the client. There are several situations that justify developing a new solution.

➤ There is nothing currently available on the market that meets the client requirements.

➤ The new solution offers crucial advantages in strategic business areas.

➤ The project has the required skills and experience to handle a nonstandard solution.

➤ It strategically exceeds the client's competitors.

➤ It offers business advantages that are sustainable over time.

➤ Re-engineering the process to work with a standard solution is not appropriate or represents a high risk.

➤ The new solution provides a clear market differentiation.

## ➤ Outsourcing

One of the options open to project managers is to outsource either (a) part or (b) the entire project to an external contractor. There are a number of reasons why this might look like an attractive option. The decision to outsource to a third party or contractor stems from the realization that the skills and knowledge to achieve a successful outcome do not, and should not, reside in the client's capabilities.

It is important to recognize that outsourcing does not reduce risk unless the outsource requirements are clear to both the client and the contractor. The contractor, on one hand, must provide the necessary skills to manage such outsourcing contracts. The client, on the other hand, must decide if its information technology activities are not core competencies. The client must also decide if it is seeking to lower its long-term capital investment, thereby moving unwanted technical risks and management problems onto a contractor who has the capacity to deal with them.

Even today, countries such as China, India, and the Philippines possess impressive ultramodern IT infrastructures, skills, and resources to tackle IT projects, completely offshore. Table 4.9 identifies some of the factors affecting outsourcing.

## ➤ Project Go / No Go Decision

After the analysis and feasibility of the project have been completed and verified for accuracy, the executive team has

**Table 4.9**  Outsourcing IT to contractors

| Benefits of Outsourcing | Disadvantages of Outsourcing |
| --- | --- |
| Lower cost—cheaper to develop or maintain | Legal disputes |
| | Contractual abuse |
| Faster development—reduced time to market | Additional administration due to travel, meetings |
| Skilled and certified IT resources | |
| Risk managed by outsource contractor | |

an opportunity to review the information that was gathered during the analysis phase. This executive team may sit as a committee, or an individual may make the decision. The go/no go decision will determine whether a project is worth pursuing. The following are some types of questions can be raised:

➤ Does the project or opportunity have the required funding or budget?

➤ Can the project be delivered at an acceptable business risk to the organization?

➤ What are the chances (e.g., 90 percent) of delivering the project on time?

➤ Are the appropriate resources available to perform the project, and, if not, can they be obtained?

➤ When will the client be expected to proceed with the project (e.g., 60 days, 120 days)?

➤ What is the likely ROI and estimated profitability that can be expected on the project?

Remember that it is up to the project manager to ensure that the business analysis of the proposed solution is completed and that it reaches the decision makers in the organization for a go/no go decision. The following decisions can be made:

➤ The overall project is approved and the start of the next phase can commence (GO).

➤ The project is returned as incomplete until additional aspects have been covered (NO GO).

➤ The project is rejected due to the results stated within the analysis (NO GO).

➤ **Analysis Kick-off Meeting**

The project manager, together with the business analyst, should always insist on an initial formal kick-off meeting with the client and identified client staff members. The purpose of the meeting is to determine the requirements of the solution and to document expectations, goals, and success criteria. The kick-off meeting should be conducted with initial high-level project stakeholders at the beginning of the project. The output of the meeting is to articulate management objectives, produce the draft project charter document, produce the work breakdown structure, and establish the strategic schedule (see Figure 4.7).

# ■ LESSONS LEARNED DURING THE ANALYSIS PHASE

On any project, the managing risks and problems could be simplified if lessons could be learned from previous projects (see Figure 4.8). The following list attempts to highlight some of these problems:

➤ Complex projects have a reputation of delivering benefits late and come in over budget.

KICK-OFF MEETING

- Welcome / Introduction
- Project overview
- Discuss project scope
- High-Level project deliverables
- Member roles & responsibilities
- Discuss communication on project
- Discuss frequency of meetings
- General discussion—open
- Next meeting

Client / end-User

Procurement
manager

Project sponsor

Quality
assurance

Project manager

Development manager

Business / Systems
analyst

IT help desk

Maintenance & support

Configuration
manager / coordinator

**Figure 4.7**  Project kick-off meeting involvement

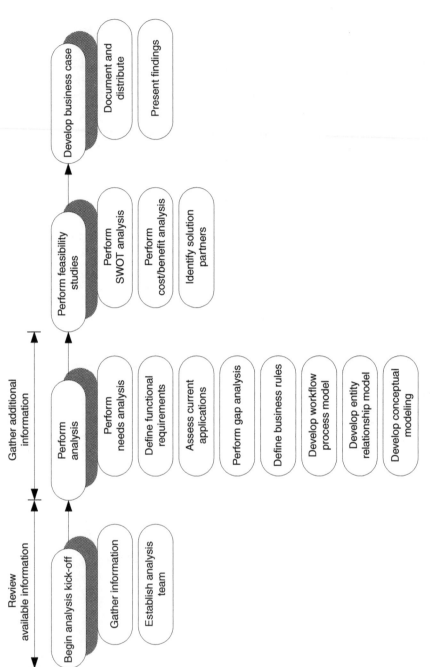

**Figure 4.8** Overview of analysis tasks

➤ The most effective way of containing risk during the startup phase of the project is to use experienced and skilled people.

➤ Document everything. A set of complete documentation will minimize uncertainty and ensure easier updating when making revisions to either requirements or estimates.

➤ When dealing across organizational boundaries, always ensure that you define and clarify roles and responsibilities of the project (i.e., who is responsible for what task).

➤ The lack of support, confidence, or excitement on the part of the client or sponsor could be a symptom that something is wrong.

➤ The business analysis should include averages and peaks in the documented analysis when reviewing the system. If the system is not designed to meet peak demands, then it will fail.

## ➤ I Wish I Had Known That

The following risks highlight possible problem areas that could impede or make the overall project more problematic. Project managers need to ask several questions in order to avoid serious problems.

➤ Does the project have committed analysts?

➤ Is there a project manager or analyst responsible for delivering the business benefits?

➤ Is there an experienced project manager?

➤ Is there an agreed upon analysis process?

➤ Is there a detailed plan for project management, including allocation of project responsibilities, accountability, and authority levels? Do project staff understand and accept the business objectives and proposed technology?

➤ Do the analysts have experience documenting and capturing data?

➤ Have the analysts assessed similar projects before?

➤ Consultation is needed not only with existing and potential users of the system, but also with those who originate and use the information being processed. Are the customers and users of the system committed to the analysis and resulting statement of their needs?

## ➤ Phase Completion Checklist

The project manager should ensure that the following project documentation is filed within the main project folder in order to complete the project analysis phase:

➤ Client contract or letter of intent

➤ User requirement specification

➤ Project proposal

➤ Business case

➤ Terms of reference

➤ Feasibility study

➤ Project work authorization

➤ Analysis worksheets and data

➤ Status reports

➤ Minutes of the meeting

➤ Any inbound and outbound correspondence

➤ All final project costs, such as timesheets, invoices, and so forth

# Chapter 5

# Planning for Success

## ■ PLANNING BEGINS

The core function of the project manager during the planning phase is to plan and provide a roadmap for the project. Proper planning is the cornerstone of a successful project, while improper planning is often the primary cause of a failed project. There are a few important steps that are part of planning a good project. The primary focus of project planning is to identify the following:

➤ What needs to be done?

➤ How complex is the project?

➤ When it will be done?

➤ How will it be done?

➤ Who will be responsible for each task?

➤ What types of deliverables will be needed?

➤ What skillsets and quantity of resources are needed?

➤ How much will the project cost?

Early project planning brings relevant issues, points of disagreement, assumptions, and risks to the table in order that they be resolved immediately. Because plans are established early on in the project, the project manager will face many unknowns and must deal with them accordingly. These assumptions are always documented as part of the plan. Later on, as the assumptions are resolved, the plan can be modified appropriately.

> *After you have determined your plans, cause the officers to know them. Knowledgeable officers can be trusted. Make rewards clear and then the troops will advance without hesitation.* —Sun Tzu

Planning relies on three critical elements: (1) good input, (2) good planning, and (3) proper allocation of needed resources. For the project manager, planning is about deciding which activities have to take place and when, as well as allocating resources to allow the meeting of deadlines. Can you imagine a project being planned without any prior specifications and blueprints? I think not!

For over ten years, I have worked in IT project management on different types of IT projects. During that time, I developed many different planning methods and techniques that contributed to the success of a project. I have also seen many project managers dive straight into the development phase, developing software or products, without the appropriate planning in place. When the project ran into problems, it was often too late to turn back, and these projects often failed in some way. In cases where no planning was done, it became extremely difficult to reverse such a situation.

It is essential that a considerable amount of time be spent planning a project. It is extremely likely that the project manager will be required to double-check the project planning in order to reflect last-minute changes and unforeseen circumstances taking shape on the project. A project manager can quickly determine how difficult a task he or she will face based on the results of the initial planning. Figure 5.1 illustrates a basic planning process.

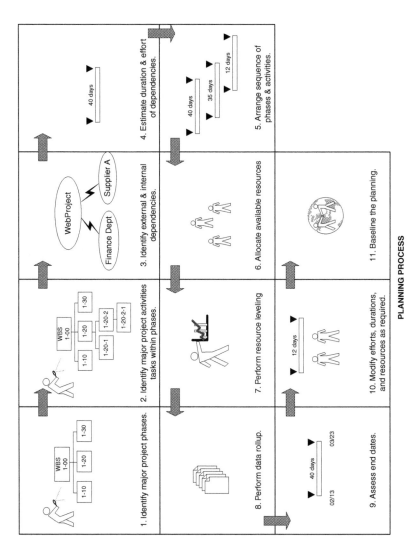

**PLANNING PROCESS**

1. Identify major project phases.

2. Identify major project activities tasks within phases.

3. Identify external & internal dependencies.

4. Estimate duration & effort of dependencies.

5. Arrange sequence of phases & activities.

6. Allocate available resources

7. Perform resource leveling

8. Perform data rollup.

9. Assess end dates.

10. Modify efforts, durations, and resources as required.

11. Baseline the planning.

**Figure 5.1**   Planning phase activities

## ➤ Identifying the Project

Any project being planned at this stage needs to be clearly identified and allocated a unique name (e.g., Project Aspen) or a sequential tracking number (e.g., P15724) by which all stakeholders can identify and reference the particular project. The main reason for giving the project an identifier is to ensure that any related project costs (in whichever project phase) are clearly carried against that specific project. Could you imagine the effort involved in trying to explain to a finance department which costs should be carried against? I doubt this would be an easy task for any project manager or administrator.

The benefit of being able to track a project is clearly evident. It aids not only communication, but also auditing and archiving. Let's assume that a particular project is one of many being managed for a certain client. Each year, this client is required to undergo a financial auditing process. When a discrepancy is discovered on a specific cost item, neither the auditors nor the client are able to trace the item to the correct project. This makes a complex and time-consuming administrative burden for all involved. To this end, assigning a name to a project is advised for any project manager.

## ➤ Keeping Things Simple

Wherever possible, ask the question "How can we reduce the complexity of this project?" In IT projects modifying existing systems and software significantly increases complexity and risk: A complex project takes longer, and this makes it inherently more risky than a simpler one. One way to gain a measure of control is to break down software requirements into smaller, more manageable pieces with defined outputs to be delivered within short time scales.

When dealing with the integration of various technologies as delivered by multiple suppliers, it becomes easier for the project manager to have one prime contractor responsible for the total integration. Organizations are depending more on their IT systems to achieve success. It is therefore vital that new systems are integrated into the business quickly and effectively. However, successfully integrating new IT systems with existing systems and business processes is one of the key problem areas for many organizations.

# ■ INITIAL PLANNING

In order to establish the initial planning for the project and to gain a better understanding of what needs to occur, the project manager needs to obtain all prior business analysis and reference documentation. The following are suggested steps for basic planning:

1. Create the initial project management plan.

2. Determine the duration and level of effort of the proposed work.

3. Ensure that all constraints and assumptions have been included.

4. Achieve consensus with stakeholders for all tasks and durations.

5. Create the initial staffing requirements.

The main planning steps taken for project planning also need to be executed as part of the overall planning. Table 5.1 lists the main tasks that need to be performed.

**Table 5.1** Main project planning tasks

| Plan | Techniques Used |
|------|-----------------|
| Develop the WBS | Functional project decomposition, software tools |
| Determine activity dependencies | Project network diagram |
| Identify project risks | Risk software, assumptions |
| Identify project milestones | WBS |
| Estimate the effort | Resource usage spreadsheets |
| Create project schedule | WBS |
| Perform project estimate | Parametric modeling |

## ➤ Work Breakdown Structure (WBS)

Time and time again, project managers get caught up with the notion that every conceivable task should be included in the development of the project WBS. The end result is a big list of tasks that does not reflect what the project manager will be doing. Building a WBS for a major project can be time-consuming but well worth it.

I have seen many project managers produce wonderful and complex WBS documents that leave their seniors admiring the detail and staggering results the document describes. Due to the complexity and type of integration that projects require today, project managers need to rely on the SMEs and technical specialists because there is no chance that the project manager will think of everything.

Milestones are those physical elements that the project will deliver. The WBS should reflect the major project milestones as well as their associated target dates. Some of the possible deliverables a project manager should consider are project plans and important documentation (e.g., billing specification, user manuals) and physical products (e.g., hardware, modules, training, etc.).

The WBS is a hierarchical grouping of project elements (similar to a family tree), starting with the higher levels and breaking these down into lower-level elements. The WBS can be viewed in either tabular linear format or in graphical format. The underlying rule of the WBS is to break the project down into small, manageable parts, whereby owners for each deliverable are established. Once this has been completed, the project manager estimates the cost for each task (see Figure 5.2). There are six commonly used steps used to build a WBS.

1. Determine the high-level phases of the project.

2. Separate these high-level phases into detailed work packages.

3. Arrange the tasks in logical order or sequence.

4. Estimate the task duration and the effort for each task.

5. Review the WBS with all stakeholders.

6. Incorporate any changes to the WBS and baseline the WBS.

## ➤ Product Breakdown Structure (PBS)

Often projects are established to develop a specific product (e.g., mobile phone). The technique used to identify and represent the physical and functional breakdown of a product is known as the product breakdown structure (PBS). Within the systems management world, it is known as the bill of materials (BOM). It is good to be able to develop a PBS for the product, as this will aid the project manager in identifying major deliverables for the project. Figure 5.3 is an example of a PBS.

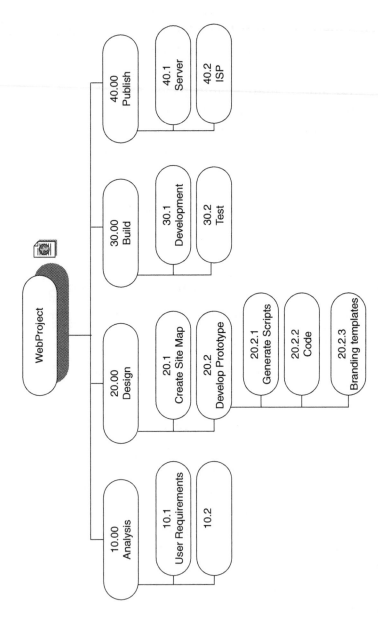

**Figure 5.2**  The work breakdown structure (WBS) chart

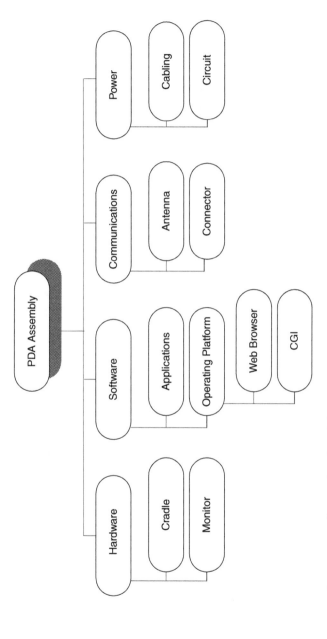

**Figure 5.3**    The product breakdown structure (PBS) chart

## ➤ Project Schedule Preparation (Gantt Chart)

The development of an overall project schedule can be conducted using a Gantt chart, the most commonly used tool for displaying project schedules. It allows for a clear snapshot of the project at a glance. There are numerous project scheduling software tools available on the market today that allow the project manager to create a schedule, allocate resources, and identify the critical path. However, in creating the Gantt chart, the project manager needs to understand how to create a basic chart. The minimum information shown displayed on a Gantt chart consists of:

➤ A horizontal time scale displaying the project by days, months, or years

➤ A list of project activities and milestones displayed vertically on the left-hand side of the chart

➤ Allocation of manpower and material resources to each activity

➤ Proportional bar indicating the duration of each activity indicated on the horizontal axis

I have always found it useful to follow some process when developing the Gantt or schedule, and I use a seven-step process to assist me in creating the project schedule (see Figure 5.4).

1. Review the project calendar (to identify holidays, vacations, etc.).

2. Assess the time constraints on the project (e.g., completion date, dependencies, etc.).

3. Start sequencing the tasks (e.g., logical progression of tasks).

| ID | Task Name | Start | End | Duration | Resource Name | Percent Complete |
|----|-----------|-------|-----|----------|---------------|------------------|
| 1 | Task 1 | 1/9/2002 | 2/5/2002 | 4w | Project Manager | 100% |
| 2 | Task 2 | 2/6/02 | 4/15/2002 | 9w 4d | Analyst | 50% |
| 3 | Task 3 | 4/16/02 | 8/15/2002 | 17w 3d | Developers | 0% |
| 4 | Task 4 | 3/12/02 | 4/26/2002 | 6w 4d | Supplier | 50% |
| 5 | Task 5 | 5/21/2002 | 8/5/2002 | 11w | Tester, QA | 0% |
| 6 | Task 6 | 8/27/02 | 9/16/2002 | 3w | Stakeholders | 0% |
| 7 | Task 7 | 9/17/02 | 9/17/2002 | 0w | Project manager | 0% |

**Figure 5.4**  Preparing the schedule

4. Determine the resources needed (e.g., identify skills, technologies, budget, etc.).

5. Estimate the task duration(s) and verify time involved per task.

6. Identify the shortest route from start to finish between tasks (i.e., the critical path).

7. Develop the project schedule using the above steps.

However, while preparing the Gantt chart, it is important to understand the relationship between project activities. Dependencies that are incorrectly estimated will influence the entire schedule from now onward, and the project manager may have to start the schedule over. Remember that the relationship between two activities is where one activity depends on the start or finish of another activity in order to begin or end. The activity that depends on the other activity is the successor and the task it depends upon is the predecessor. Figure 5.5 shows the dependencies commonly used when creating a schedule.

In the process of developing the project schedule, it is common for some project durations to be unknown, and guessing isn't entirely accurate either. Maybe too much padding has been added or the duration has been reduced by too many days or even weeks. This assessment is often unrealistic and dishonest. In the event that the above values cannot be estimated, then the project manager should rely on the expertise of the SMEs to assist with estimating the duration. They will be able to provide more accurate values to use in calculating the average duration for a project task. In this scenario, the weighted-average time technique is used in order to determine the expected average duration for a given task. The formula is as follows:

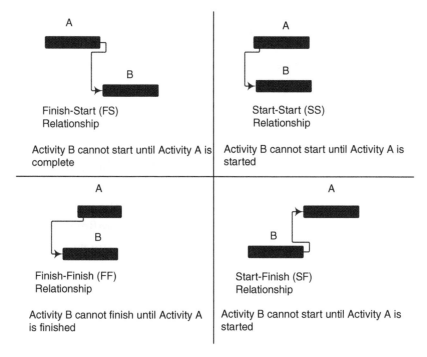

Figure 5.5   Defining task relationships

Ave Duration =

$$\frac{\text{Most Optimistic Value (4} \times \text{Most Likely Value)} + \text{Pessimistic Value}}{6}$$

Projects that exceed cost and time due to bad estimates can cause the company to face financial losses. The consequences include lost business opportunities and failure to bringing the product to market ahead of the competition. Accurate estimates reduce the risk of project overruns, thereby sharply curtailing negative business effects. This is why so many businesses are relying on the parametric based estimates. Accurately estimating project costs and schedules is vital in determining the success of a project.

## ➤ Arrow Network Diagram Technique

A technique that I have found that really assists project managers in sequencing project activities, identifying gaps, and identifying possible dependency relationships is the arrow network diagram technique. In many cases, a project manager literally cannot see the forest for the trees; problems start arising later on the project when he or she realizes that there are, in fact, dependencies that had not been recognized, and the sequence was done incorrectly. Therefore, it is important to have a simple technique to reflect dependencies in graphic form. However, there are some rules to this graphing technique.

➤ The network diagram is always drawn from left to right.

➤ It is not drawn to scale.

➤ An arrow represents an activity, with the tail indicating the start and the arrowhead its completion.

➤ Arrows must follow the sequence of the work to be done.

➤ The length of the arrow is not important.

➤ The start and end points of an activity are called events and are represented by circles.

➤ The events are usually labeled with a number (1, 2, etc.).

➤ Broken-line arrows represent dummy activities and show where one activity depends on another.

Using these rules, the activity network is built to allow for some adjustments and refinement of the network where

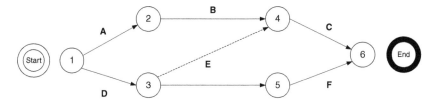

**Figure 5.6** Arrow network diagram

needed (see Figure 5.6). It may be the case that activities are either to be deleted or reassessed. The network is built in the following way.

1. *List all activities.* Separate the project into a list of activities, depending upon the size of the project and desired depth. Use the WBS as a reference tool.

2. *Sequence the activities.* Start sequencing all the activities in their correct order and include the applicable activity dependencies that apply to them. Remember to look at those activities that must be completed before the next activity can begin as well as those activities that can start at the same time.

## ➤ Project Critical Path

In essence, the critical path is a technique for calculating the total duration of a project based on a specified start date and on the individual duration of activities and their dependencies upon one another. Remember that if there is an activity on this critical path that gets delayed, then the project is delayed—pushing the project status into red, and that is not where anyone wants to be. For all those activities that are not on the critical path, it means that the project manager is okay and can be more flexible with those specific tasks. Understanding exactly how one gets to a critical path is somewhat tricky. First, the project manager needs to create a well-documented network diagram. There are a host of software packages that can be used to do this, and some create it very quickly. Once the project manager has the network diagram, he or she simply adds each parallel path's activities together; the path that requires the longest time to run through the project is the critical path. This means that it is the *shortest time* in which the project can be completed.

Once the project manager has determined the critical path, it is very important to monitor this path and understand that, if the activities start slipping on the critical path, it is highly likely that the overall project may start failing. To reduce the project time, the project manager should allocate more resources to those activities on the critical path.

# ■ PROJECT ESTIMATION

Predicting the outcome of any project is difficult because there are numerous methods for estimating what a project would cost. Projects that are similar and have historical data are easier for the project manager to estimate, compared to projects that are unique in nature and have never been attempted before. While there is no such thing as a reliable estimate, there are realistic ones. An accurate estimate reduces the risk of project overruns, thus sharply curtailing negative affects on business. Estimating is a skill that improves over time, and project managers should not initially attempt to do any estimation work without guidance from experienced project estimators or cost accountants. Without accurate estimates, the following scenario will occur:

➤ Your project will be behind schedule—thus late.

➤ Your project will be over budget—thus have cost overruns.

➤ You will likely lose your client—because you can't meet client expectations.

## ➤ The Estimation Process

The project manager should remember that the estimation that results from the planning phase is not final and is considered a temporary estimate. Once more detailed project planning is performed and the project costs and WBS schedules are fine-tuned, a more accurate estimate emerges. Basically, the estimation process has a few primary steps:

1. Develop the WBS.

2. Estimate each part of the WBS constituting the total project.

3. Schedule the work according to each WBS task.

4. Determine the resources needed, quantities, and availability.

5. Obtain the latest resource rates, including next salary reviews and increases.

6. Determine the level of effort needed to complete each WBS task.

Something that is very important during the estimation process is that project managers ask the client to pay a price that is relevant to the perceived value of what they receive. If the client is willing to pay for the project, the project manager needs to determine whether it is profitable enough to do the work. To determine this, project managers must determine cost. This is where the estimation is needed (see Table 5.2).

Figure 5.7 illustrates the typical project costs that should be considered.

**Table 5.2**  What to include in a project estimate

| Project Cost Estimate | Description |
| --- | --- |
| Internal labor or cost of employees | Burdened cost to company — benefits included |
| Hardware costs | Servers, printers, workstations |
| Software and licensing | Application software, downloaded software patches, code |
| Travel and accommodation | Airfares, hotel, tolls, gas |
| Administrative support costs | Personnel, finance, and legal support |
| Training costs | User training, computer-based training, lesson plans |
| System documentation costs | Manuals, policy & procedures, on-line documentation |
| Stationary costs | Project stationary |
| Infrastructure costs | Office space, desks, rent, parking |

## ➤ Estimating the Effort

It is said that you cannot manage what you cannot measure. No matter what project a project manager has been allocated or assigned too, the project estimate should include the following:

- ➤ Size of the project
- ➤ Resources required
- ➤ Project duration
- ➤ Costs needed to complete the project, labor, hardware, travel, etc.

Estimates in the IT industries are incredibly difficult to complete due to so many unknowns. The initial estimate is, in many ways, the most important. The initial estimate will be a focal point with which the project manager can compare

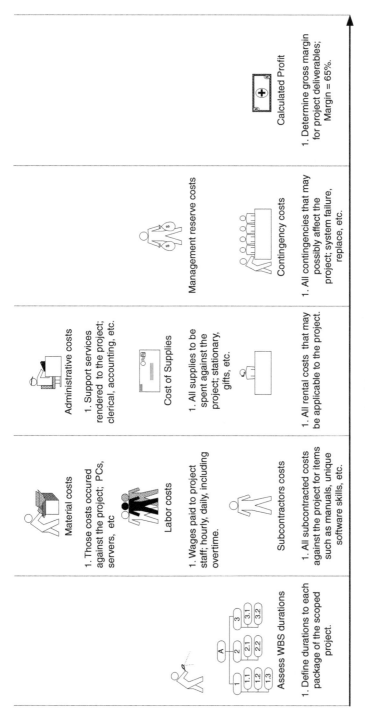

**Figure 5.7** Consolidating project costs

**ASSESSING PROJECT COSTS**

**Assess WBS durations**

1. Define durations to each package of the scoped project.

**Material costs**

1. Those costs occured against the project; PCs, servers, etc

**Labor costs**

1. Wages paid to project staff; hourly, daily, including overtime.

**Subcontractors costs**

1. All subcontracted costs against the project for items such as manuals, unique software skills, etc.

**Administrative costs**

1. Support services rendered to the project; clerical, accounting, etc.

**Cost of Supplies**

1. All supplies to be spent against the project; stationary, gifts, etc.

1. All rental costs that may be applicable to the project.

**Management reserve costs**

**Contingency costs**

1. All contingencies that may possibly affect the project; system failure, replace, etc.

**Calculated Profit**

1. Determine gross margin for project deliverables; Margin = 65%.

all future estimates. Because of this, there are several recommended steps to follow when achieving an initial estimate.

- ➤ Break down the project requirements as far as possible to subsystem levels (WBS).

- ➤ For each WBS element, identify its similarities with previously developed projects and use this historical data.

- ➤ For those WBS element units not strongly related to previous IT projects, use SMEs to estimate the size of those elements needed.

- ➤ Form the size estimate for the entire project by rolling up the estimates for all the WBS elements.

- ➤ From historical data and expertise, estimate the level of effort.

- ➤ Divide the size estimate by the work rate to obtain an estimate of the effort in work hours.

Once the WBS has been developed, many project managers move directly to determining the duration of the task. This is normally done using a software tool, and it visually appears as though the project manager is on the right track. This is not the correct approach; it creates room for errors and bad planning. Remember that it takes a lot of skill and experience to estimate all WBS tasks. For example, it can take one seasoned IT architect a few hours to do a server capacity assessment, but the same task could take two junior IT architects double the amount of time to perform.

Similarly, a situation may arise where only one person can do a specific task, such as cloning a server. Only one resource can do the specific task, not two. Therefore, in this

**Table 5.3**   Parametric modeling

| Description of an IT Project | | Value | |
| --- | --- | --- | --- |
| Java developers | (100 hours x $90 / hour) | $9,000.00 | |
| System administrator | (10 hours x $60 / hour) | $ 600.00 | |
| Webmaster | (20 hours x $80 / hour) | $1,200.00 | |
| **Total Direct Cost**—(The burdened labor cost is excluded—no benefits, overheads included.) | | $10,800.00 | **A** |
| We now include the burdened labor rate if determined to be = 1.08 | | $11,664.00 | **B** |
| **Total Direct Cost for Project** | | $22,464.00 | **A + B** |

case, the emphasis is on ensuring that the resource is best-qualified to perform this task. The project manager also needs to discuss the issue with an SME to determine the amount of effort. The cost per task is directly related to the resources and effort needed. The project manager must accommodate the level of effort needed to perform the task.

## ➤ Top-down Estimating (Parametric)

The WBS forms the basis of the top-down estimation technique. Here the focus is on the project manager identifying those project parameters that indicate what the project resources will cost. This is an opportunity to break down the costs of the project from the top working downward, and thus having a visual representation of all project values. Table 5.3 shows an example of top-down estimation.

## ➤ Bottom-up Estimating

This technique relies heavily on the WBS approach. It is a useful method, often used due to its accuracy and ability to roll up the project costs from the lowest level to the higher levels by referencing it against the WBS. Both time and cost

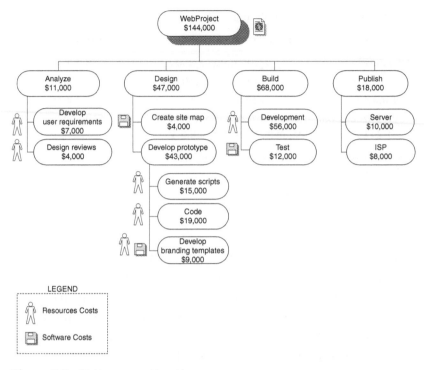

**Figure 5.8** Bottom up estimating

are allocated against each WBS item, and SMEs provide specialist input. When this process is completed, the costs roll up to each subsequent higher level. Eventually, a total project cost is determined (see Figure 5.8). It must be noted that it can be difficult to use this method on a project where the scope was not fully determined (i.e., Research and Development—R&D project).

## ➤ Phased Estimating

It is probable that the technological nature of many projects, such as R&D projects, makes it extremely difficult to estimate the entire project effort accurately. In these circumstances, the only approach still open to the project manager is to provide a project estimate on a phase-by-phase basis.

This is often difficult for a client to accept, let alone understand, as the client requires the complete project dollar value for cash flow and budgetary purposes. To this end, it often appears to the client that the project team is unwilling to accept the project risk.

Phased estimating can actually be in the client's best financial interest due to the fact that the client is now able to review each project phase at specific intervals. In reality, the client remains in full control and could either stop or reject the project at any stage if unsatisfactory results seem likely. For example, let's assume that an investor has asked a software company to develop a portable, handheld, medical artificial intelligence unit that can perform automated medical diagnosis for both human and animal life forms in real-time. The project manager, during the estimation process, would identify this project as a pure R&D project, and because of the undeveloped technology and applications required, would recommend that this project be estimated on a phase-by-phase basis.

## ➤ Accuracy of Estimation

Because accuracy is so important when planning a good project, I normally use both the top-down and bottom-up estimating techniques to evaluate the results I have achieved. If the results are similar, then I know that I'm on the right track. If, however, the results vary considerably, then it means something is wrong, and I may need to review the values again. This time, I will solicit expert judgement by using a certified cost accountant or seasoned project manager to go through the estimation with me.

## ➤ Estimating Profit

Once the project manager has determined the resources he or she will be using on the project and against which WBS tasks, it becomes necessary for that project manager to calculate the selling rate for each resource being used on the project. It is logical to assume that the project manager cannot sell the resources at the same price the company does, and a suitable markup needs to be applied against each resource type. Some issues that need to be considered before adding values to any resource include the following:

➤ The project manager should ensure that he or she has the latest resource rates from the human resource department or consultant manager (e.g., Java developer costs $90.00 per hour — burdened).

➤ The project manager should ensure that he or she has obtained the costs of hardware and software and has determined the company markup rate for these items (e.g., the markup on software will be 15 percent in addition to the price from which it was obtained).

➤ The project manager should determine which resources are due for salary increases, which can affect the project rates.

➤ The project manager should obtain the markup rate or percent from the finance department.

➤ To calculate the gross margin of the project, determine the difference between the selling rate and the direct cost to company, less disbursements.

➤ **The Project Office Role in Estimates**

I have found that large corporations and organizations use project offices to assist project managers in ensuring that their project estimates are correct and have been reviewed before being released to a client. Some of these services are:

**Table 5.4** Resource skills required by project

| WBS # | Project Resource | Qty | Skills Required |
|---|---|---|---|
| 1.2 | Project manager | 1 | Project management, ASP, HTML, Word |
| 2.3 | Business analyst | 2 | Database skills, Excel, Word, |
| 3.0 | Developers | 3 | IIS4.0, ASP, JavaScript, HTML, PERL |
| 4.2 | Tester | 1 | Word, Test case development |
| 5.0 | Trainer | 1 | Presentation skills, PowerPoint, CBT |

➤ Verifying and validating the WBS and estimate — tightening the estimation effort or identifying sloppy planning

➤ Supplying the services of a central pool of cost accountants or subject matter experts

➤ Maintaining the historical database of completed project estimates and WBS charts

➤ Assisting in the presentation or recommending the project estimates for approval

## ➤ Planning and Selecting Project Resources

It is critical to the planning stage that the project manager determines exactly what type of resources will be needed to design, develop, test, and implement a specific project. A vital task of the project manager is to select team resources who are well-qualified to perform the work of the IT project. The project manager must identify the technical, interpersonal, and organizational skills needed to complete the project. One technique to determine this requirement is to create a first-pass skills assessment matrix for the project (see Table 5.4).

The project manager is the focal point of contact in identifying the necessary skill levels. The following steps can help project managers determine the resources needed on the project:

➤ Ensure the project WBS is approved and that all tasks are in order and correctly identified.

➤ Assess each WBS activity by the core skillsets needed (i.e., analysts, developers, testers).

➤ Assess the quantity resources that would be needed per WBS activity to shorten the duration.

➤ Document each resource skillset with estimated quantities needed.

Planning involves understanding how the company's human resource policies and guidelines will affect the project. All project stakeholders must know and understand their roles in the project, which all contribute to the success of the project.

When dealing with any part-time or temporary resources on the project, project managers should be aware that the project gains the maximum value from part-time individuals assigned to the project. So very often, part-time members are recalled back to their previous projects on urgent matters, and never return. This leads to frustration, as these recalled resources are now unable to work the time that has been dedicated to the project. In order to do the resource planning on the project, it is necessary to have some base information to get good results. Possible sources for this information are

➤ Historical information from a similar project

➤ Knowledge from within the organization

➤ Benchmark information from other organizations

**Table 5.5**  Planning for resource usage

| Resource Type | Qty | Part-time/ Contractor | Rate | Required Hours | Cost ($) |
|---|---|---|---|---|---|
| Project manager | 1 | ✓ | $120 | 160 | $19,200.00 |
| Business analyst | 2 | ✗ | $90 | 60 | $10,800.00 |
| Developers | 3 | ✓ | $110 | 250 | $82,500.00 |
| Tester | 1 | ✗ | $80 | 40 | $ 3,200.00 |
| Trainer | 1 | ✓ | $70 | 36 | $ 2,520.00 |
| Total Cost | 8 | 3 | | 546 hrs | $118,220.00 |

Table 5.5 illustrates a resource usage technique that allows the project manager to determine the number of resources that are required and helps the project manager understand the importance of the individual financial impacts on the project.

## ➤ Linear Responsibility Chart (LRC)

So many times, project managers are unsure of which resources to assign to which WBS task, resulting in communication and coordination problems between project stakeholders. A useful technique to aid the project manager is the linear responsibility chart (LRC) or matrix. It basically combines the WBS against the types of resources available. This is extremely useful for the project manager, as it visually depicts who is responsible for each project task. The following are suggested steps to follow when creating a LRC:

1. Document the project WBS in a linear manner on the left-hand side of the matrix.

2. Arrange all the resource elements from the corporation horizontally across the top of the matrix.

3. Assess each intersection point on the matrix to indicate each resources interest in the respective WBS activities.

Had Columbus paid closer attention to the works of the ancient Greeks, he might have noticed the reference to a landmass extending from north to south in the Atlantic Ocean, between Europe and Asia. He might also have consulted with Basque fishermen, who were already harvesting schools of cod off the coast of Labrador. Acquiring knowledge — on projects — may just be a matter of knowing where to find it. Valuable lessons like these often highlight the importance of recognizing the task at hand and put things into perspective.

## ➤ Project Budget

The detailed project budget, which the project manager forwards to the client, is final and should be the benchmark from which all costs are tracked and coordinated. This value forms the basis against which the project manager should measure the planned versus actual costs.

Many clients will fund projects basing them on their financial calendar year. Therefore, projects either have to be completed within that year, or the budget split into two separate financial years to address the client's financial commitment. The project manager needs to be well versed in the client's budgetary process, in order to gain understanding of how to submit invoicing or generate credit notes, if needed.

The final budget is derived from the most recent estimate approved by the project manager and the relevant senior stakeholders. Once verified and approved, the budget is forwarded to the client for project approval. It would be very unprofessional to inform the client that the budget was not realistic and still needed fine-tuning. Remember that a good project manager will only commit to a schedule or budget if he or she knows it can be met. Table 5.6 shows an example of a project and monthly budget.

**Table 5.6**  Project budget and monthly budget ($)

| Project WBS | Value | July | August | September | October |
|---|---|---|---|---|---|
| A | $19,200.00 | $4,000.00 | $4,000.00 | $4,000.00 | $7,200.00 |
| B | $10,800.00 | | $10,800.00 | | |
| C | $82,500.00 | | | $60,000.00 | $22,500.00 |
| D | $ 3,200.00 | | | | $3,200.00 |
| E | $ 2,520.00 | | | | $2,520.00 |
| **Total Budget** | $118,220.00 | $4,000.00 | $14,800.00 | $64,000.00 | $35,420.00 |

# ■ PROJECT COSTING MODELS

It is essential that project managers understand the importance of the types of financial contracts a client could impose on the project or ones that the project manager could recommend to the client. Without a doubt, if the project manager is responsible for the financial success of the project, he or she needs to understand how these contracts work. To move ahead without comprehending the contract will, undoubtedly, affect the financial aspect of this project and it will most certainly fail.

Most projects are formally agreed upon and executed by means of a contract. If a project does not proceed according to plan, the client often has several choices: (1) recover what they can from the project and never do business with the consulting company again, (2) request the project be delivered as agreed, or (3) continue with legal proceedings.

Certain financial contracts could negatively affect the planned project profits, which would result in a project coming in at a loss to the company. There are also some financial contracts that could be beneficial if project performance is achieved. This section describes the risks associated with each of the major types of financial contracts that I have often seen used on IT projects. Basically there are two main contract models to consider; firm fixed price (FFP) and cost plus (CP)

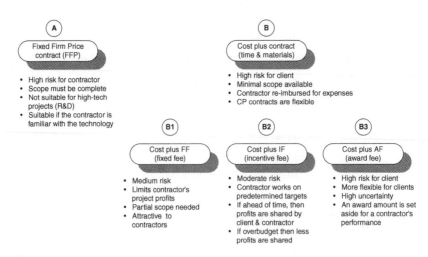

**Figure 5.9**   Costing models

(also more commonly known as a time and materials contract). The CP model has a few variations that are applied depending on client negotiations, but all have been used.

I shall not go into great detail about all the types of contracts that are available for a project manager to consider and understand, but I will highlight those that I believe are useful (see Figure 5.9).

## ➤ Firm Fixed-Price Contracts

This type of contract favors the project manager and the solution provider, even though the risk is placed on the solution provider to deliver against what was quoted. This risk works well if the project manager has a superior knowledge of the solution type being undertaken. If the project manager cannot deliver the solution as quoted, then the solution provider, not the client, accommodates the risk.

For example, let's assume the client approves a quote of $126K for a project. However, at project completion the costs exceed the $150K mark, and the project manager must explain why such a loss occurred. The client will not pay the difference, as they only agreed to the $126K quote. However, if the project is managed successfully and can achieve the required gross margin (profit margin), the solution provider will be extremely satisfied and it often happens that project managers get suitably compensated for achieving these financial margins.

## ➤ Time-and-Materials Contracts

A time-and-materials contract places the risk with the client. This type of contract is often used when the contractor or project manager is unsure of quoting an FFP, as the solution may be (1) too complex, (2) at a client's request, or (3) used in order to supplement project staff on a project.

This form of contract is usually administered when project managers submit their invoices to the client to receive payment for work-hours and physical materials used on the project (e.g., stationary, hotel stays, and other related costs). These contracts do consume larger portions of administrative burden for both the client and contractor.

For the contractor, the gross margins do, in some instances, tend to be lower. In these cases the common tactic is to negotiate with the client to keep the resources for longer duration, which obviously is more beneficial to the contractor.

## ■ PROJECT DOCUMENTATION

It is important that the project have sufficient documentation to cover all relevant areas that would likely cause a risk or issue. This next section describes some plans that are important to the success of any project.

## ➤ Project Management Plan

As a project manager, I have seen plans of every size—from two-page project plans all the way to documents the size of

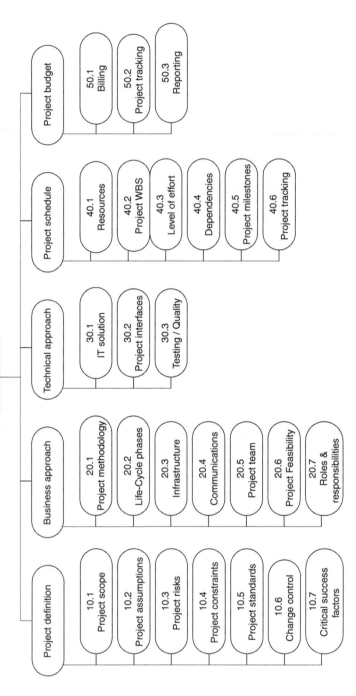

**Figure 5.10** Project plan contents

telephone directories. Some are literally so complex that very few people actually understand them. In effect, the project management plan (PMP), also known as the project definition report (PDR), is nothing more than documents describing the project that is being undertaken. It focuses on the approach to be taken, the time, cost, resources, risks, and assumptions (see Figure 5.10).

An effective project plan is of great help to the project manager because it allows individuals within the team to take more responsibility for keeping to the schedule. For instance, a developer who will not finish a task on the date planned is more likely to let the project manager know if he or she can see how this will affect the schedule.

The plan also allows everyone to have some input. For example, it allows a quality manager to determine when to schedule, and possibly begin testing earlier than expected. Because of these things, a well-communicated plan gives senior management confidence that the team as a whole knows what it is doing and can work together to bring about the project's success. The approved project plan is a formal document used to guide both project execution and project control (see Table 5.7).

By this point the project manager should be aware of the level of detail that he or she is going to present in the project plan. There are different ways of addressing the project plan, depending on whether the project is a small one or a super one. Table 5.8 presents key differences.

## ➤ Contingency Plan

The contingency plan outlines and lists the business continuity in the unlikely event that the IT project fails or disrupts the client business area or areas. A failure can be a network failure, application failure, system failure, or a complete and utter shutdown of the business. The contingency

**Table 5.7**   Project plan content

| Project Plan Content | Items Described in Content | Techniques to Be Used |
|---|---|---|
| Time | Schedules | GANTT, PERT, |
| Cost | Budgets | Top-down, Bottom–down |
| Resources | Availability of staff | Resource histogram |
|  |  | Resource loading chart |
| Required project phases | Various project phases needed | Assessment |
| Communication | Project communication | Roles & responsibilities |
| Risk | Technical, financial | Risk modeling tools |
| Administration | Project support, meetings | Organizational charts |
| Contingency plans | Backup, disaster & recovery | Assessment of solution |

plan is basically developed from the outcome of a risk analysis. All the project risks are identified, assessed, and categorized accordingly by priorities.

The project manager develops the contingency plan for the project, including a mitigation strategy for each risk that is identified. The most severe or highest priority risks are those items likely cause a major disruption to the business within a predetermined period of time (e.g., 3 hours). Nevertheless, because of the potential disruption to the business, it is vital to put a contingency plan in place, both during the project and also once the system has been commissioned and put in operation. The plan should list the critical items likely to fail and list the available resources needed to support these items. The contingency plan should list the procedures that would be necessary to permit the timely restoration of services back to normal.

The project support staff and testing teams need to be involved in the contingency planning and need to prepare items such as

Table **5.8** Project plan approach

| Small Projects | Medium to Super Projects |
|---|---|
| Milestone plan for entire project | Milestone plan for entire project |
| Single activity plan for project | Activity plan for each phase |
| | Separate plans for risk, quality, contingency, etc. |

➤ A disaster notification process and strategy

➤ Disaster recovery and backup procedures for applications and files

➤ A list of who the role players are in the event of an emergency

➤ A list of essential equipment needed to support the solution

➤ The project manager needs to be certain that a design to accommodate possible minor disruptions and an alternative backup for any major disruption that could occur are in place.

## ➤ Procurement Plan

The procurement plan describes the functions and activities that are necessary to successfully procure materials and equipment essential to project deployment. The project manager should establish procurement requirements to determine which resources should be procured externally versus internally. The procurement plan can be short and consist of only a few pages if required, but it should clearly list the intended resources needed to implement the solution. These resources could be hardware, software, leasing agreements, licensing or any other materials required on the project. The plan specifies vendor selection, acceptance of vendor deliverables, and the procurement process policy and procedures that need to be followed.

## ➤ Communication Plan

An effective communication management plan is critical to the success of a deployment project, as the project manager needs to maintain a close relationship with all parties during the project. The plan provides all project stakeholders with information regarding how resources are being used to accomplish the project objectives, and it serves as an effective tool with which to document the project owner's expectations. The information can be posted on a web site, which allows users on the project to review important documentation, schedules, and procedures. The following should be included within the project communication plan:

- ➤ All internal and external stakeholders who are expected to support the project
- ➤ A communications matrix with roles and responsibilities
- ➤ Guidelines for all information created and distributed
- ➤ Description of the project directory and filing system with access privileges
- ➤ Reporting guidelines and types of reports to be used
- ➤ Project status meetings and frequency of meetings
- ➤ Management reviews (design, budget, closure)

## ➤ Test and Quality Plan

Quality management is necessary to ensure that the project will satisfy the needs for which it was undertaken and exceed customer expectations. It describes how the project team should implement its quality policy and helps guarantee that all project team members understand that everyone is a partner in quality.

An audit should be performed periodically to verify that processes and procedures are in compliance and that the necessary quality review meetings are established to review and make corrective adjustments to the project. Checklists should be developed to ensure that project plans are complete and to eliminate the omission of items. Reports relevant to the quality management of the project should be created and distributed to all project stakeholders describing the following areas:

➤ Quality objectives within the scope of the project

➤ Quality management organization, roles, and responsibilities

➤ Documentation requirements

➤ Quality control procedures

➤ Applicable standards

➤ Tools, techniques, and methodologies to be employed

The testing manager should develop the test plan, and it should cover all anticipated testing activities. These activities should be synchronized with the overall high-level project schedule. The resources should be identified and correctly matched to the relevant tasks. This plan is beneficial for the project manager, who should be able to identify the needed testing tasks and have a good understanding of the testing process. The testing plan should be developed for each project phase and should consist of the minimum:

➤ Project objective

➤ Objective of tests being addressed in this strategy

➤ Test procedures

➤ Test configuration

➤ Test resources

➤ Test schedule

## ➤ Development Plan

The technical staff in the organization or on the project creates the development plan. In essence, the plan presents not only what the "change" will look like but also how to develop the solution in more detail. In many environments, the development plan has two main points. The first focuses more on development methods and approaches, including testing, while the second point focuses on the broader aspects of administration and control. The development plan provides a disciplined approach to organizing and managing the IT project. A successful IT development plan would include

➤ Scope of the development to be undertaken

➤ An overview of the current system or information systems environment

➤ Benchmarking other processes or systems

➤ The proposed development environment and interfaces

➤ Security considerations

➤ Development guidelines and standards that will be used

➤ Development resources required on the project

➤ Estimated schedule for the development

➤ Change control

By completing the development plan early in the planning phase of the project life cycle, the project manager, with the aid of the development manager/technical lead, can become familiar with the essential steps of organizing the development effort for the project.

1. Estimate resources.
2. Establish schedules.
3. Assemble staff.
4. Set milestones.

The development plan should concentrate on information that is unique or tailored to development activities. If standard policies, guidelines, or procedures will be applied to an aspect of the project, the plan should reference the documents in which these are defined rather than restating them in detail. Writing of the plan can begin as soon as any information about the PDR and scope becomes available.

The project manager should complete the plan by the end of the initiation phase. If items in the development plan are missing for any reason, the technical lead/development manager should indicate who will supply the outstanding information and when it will be supplied. Copies of the approved development plan should be distributed to all technical team members and identified stakeholders.

Two of the most critical resources are development resources and time. The development manager is concerned with how much time will be required to complete the project and what staffing level will be necessary over the development cycle. The technical lead/development manager usually performs both staff and time estimations, and accordingly arranges a project meeting with the project manager in order to review the schedule and resource requirements. Issues of staff size and composition over the life cycle are also considered.

If the project is relatively straightforward and has a short project life cycle, many IT projects simply combine the development plan and implementation plan. The reason is that many of the resources remain the same throughout the project, making the approach easier. In such a case, a combined plan works well. However, in the event that the project is a medium or large one, it is recommended that the development plan and the implementation plan be separated, as the development phase will most likely have many changes during the design and development, which impacts the implementation.

## ■ PROJECT INFRASTRUCTURE

When planning a project, the project manager could face the possibility that the client may not have sufficient infrastructure to accommodate the entire project team for the project. In such an event, an option to lease may be the best approach. The project manager cannot assume that the client will be providing the necessary infrastructure, and he or she needs to clarify this assumption. If the infrastructure is not negotiated with the client, and no provision is made within the accepted project budget, it is more than likely that this would affect profit starting at day one.

There are normally a few scenarios that the project manager is likely to encounter. However, it is very important to remember that there are always a few options available, and the project manager should be aware of the importance and costs associated with each option. These options are

➤ Virtual management (international or national)

➤ On-site management (at the client premises)

➤ Off-site management (at an independent or common facility used by the contractor)

➤ Offshore management (project managed totally offshore in another country)

Seasoned project managers know that trying to implement a system without the necessary workstations, hardware, and commercial software could be disastrous to any project. Effective logistics support needs to be arranged and included into the overall planning phase of the project.

Many projects have failed because the logistics were not planned for or were simply overlooked. Lead times of hardware and software are vital to the project schedule, and it is not uncommon for essential items to be delivered in months instead of the estimated few days. The slippage on the project has a huge effect on the entire project, and the person accountable for preventing slippage is the project manager. Needless to say, to keep things running smoothly, the project manager needs to be sure of several things.

➤ The hardware has been specified correctly and been documented.

➤ The delivery dates are confirmed and guaranteed.

➤ The necessary purchase orders have been completed and submitted for approval internally.

➤ The orders have been processed and placed with the supplier(s).

➤ The supplier(s) has given the delivery schedule.

➤ The assembly date and the configuration setup of the ordered items are defined.

➤ The commissioning dates for the ordered items have been confirmed.

## ➤ On-site Projects

Working on an on-site project implies that the project manager has to arrange for office space, logistics, and travel arrangements: This includes such items as parking, entry permits, and workstations. Very often, the client does not have sufficient infrastructure to fully support a project and expects the appointed project manager to arrange and finalize these matters. In this case the project manager will need to finalize these arrangements as quickly as possible and will need to communicate these requirements in advance to the administration manager at this site.

## ➤ Off-site Projects

For those projects that cannot be accommodated at the client facility due to unavailability of the necessary working environment, it is recommended that the project manager ensure that the contractor is able to provide the infrastructure needed. At times, this may be strategically beneficial for the contractor to perform the project at its site.

## ➤ Offshore Projects

Due to cost effectiveness it becomes more feasible to manage and develop a project offshore at an offshore contractor facility. Due to the high availability and nature of telecommunications and e-commerce, it becomes feasible to have projects managed completely offshore. Many organizations today outsource (1) enhancements to existing IT systems, (2) complete project design and development, or (3) complete maintenance and support to offshore facilities because of the unavailability of high-tech resources locally. Issues such as time zones and technological barriers become irrelevant if they are managed correctly. One just has to look at recent examples of U.S. organizations utilizing the IT infrastructures established in countries such as India and the Philippines.

## ➤ Establishing the Project Infrastructure

It is important that the project manager plans and sets up the necessary infrastructure prior to any project team members starting on the project. Each respective team member should have the following items established on or before the first week of starting on the project:

- ➤ Physical access to the building (either temporary or permanent). This could be in the form of (1) elevator key; (2) cardkey, (3) front door key or (4) scan entry access.

- ➤ Employee numbers in hand and employees are on payroll

- ➤ A desk and telephonic instrument

- ➤ Access to the corporate network

- ➤ Appropriate workstations and required software applications to perform work

- ➤ Access to necessary training in corporate policies and culture

- ➤ A mentor to coach these new members on the project

- ➤ The standard benefits of being on that project, such as parking permits and corporate discounts

# ■ THE TECHNICAL DESIGN

The technical phase or stage of the project is one that involves many resources and consumes many hours of careful design and verification. Without a sound technical design, you do not have a working system. It's that clear! A project manager would not want to face a situation where only certain deliverables were met, but the project failed due to technological problems that were not taken into consideration during the design phase. I hope to present project managers with a good idea of what crucial elements they should be looking for when designing the solution (see Figure 5.11).

The design phase aims to (1) outline the solution technically, and (2) consider the required resources needed to develop and implement the proposed system for the project. The project manager must ensure that there is constant discussion between the development manager and his or her technical team regarding the design of the solution in order to consider the following:(see Table 5.9).

## ➤ Developing the Design Specification

The project manager or development manager should prepare the technical specification document. One of the most important mandatory steps that the project manager should take en-

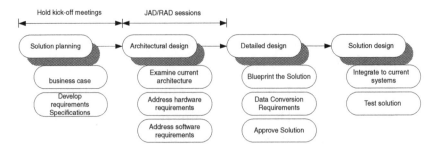

**Figure 5.11**  The technical approach

**Table 5.9** Design techniques used in the design phase

| Technique | What It Represents |
|---|---|
| Data flow model / Diagram | Flow of data for the solution |
| Entity relationship diagram (ERD) | Relationship model |
| Screen designs / User interface model | Look and feel of solution |
| Menu network / Screen navigation | Flow of the system |
| Application prototype | An exploratory model of the solution |
| System interfaces model | Definition of all the interfaces needed |
| Data dictionary | Definition of data elements in database |
| Report layouts | Definition of what the required reports are |

suring the proper completion of the design specification, in order that the technical teams will be able to understand the sequence and description of the technical tasks. Developers are expected to code their programs based upon this technical specification, and if it is incomplete, the development will certainly be behind schedule and over budget. The technical specification should meet following requirements:

➤ The client has to approve the technical specification, as it clarifies the client's requirements in technical terms. Additionally, it is used to test the programs against the approved specification.

➤ The technical specification should show all the screen layouts. This helps developers understand the required screen designs and it speeds up the development time.

➤ The technical specification should explain the functionality of each and every object/component on the required screen layouts.

➤ The technical specification should clearly indicate the required back-end technologies. For example, if a screen involves any database activities then it is good practice to show all the database tables and the appropriate actions for those tables by different objects on the screen. The rationale is that it aids in proper database design and helps the database administrator (DBA) to establish the necessary privileges on the database tables.

➤ The technical specification should also stipulate any screens that involve user input, as these need to be validated. This will help the developer to understand and code the validations in program.

Within the technical specification, the development manager, together with the SMEs, should estimate the total development time needed for the project, including time to test the solution. This will help the project manager to verify and adjust the initial time and cost estimate that was made.

The architectural design should be conceptualized and documented in order to represent the high-level design of the system. The design should address major components and system integration.

### ➤ Design Considerations

The project manager must remain involved with the technical team during the design of the entire solution. Table 5.10 presents several elements that need to be addressed during the design phase.

The project manager needs to walk away with an understanding of some key information, once the technical team has finalized their design. The project manager must be sure that

**Table 5.10** Technical specification content

| Technical Design Criteria | What Determines the Solution |
|---|---|
| Hardware specifications | Capacity |
| Application software specifications | Hardware |
| Database schema specifications | Overall architectural design |
| Telecommunications specifications | Communication |
| Peripheral devices | Performance |
| Application configuration | Operation & support |
| Interfaces | Implementation |
| Security & encryption | Security and Integration |

➤ The necessary resources have been identified per skillset

➤ The development team by the IT department can accommodate the expected start date

➤ He or she clearly understands the cost implications, if external contractors are needed to perform certain deliverables. This may imply that the project manager obtains separate cost and time estimates from these contractors.

It does happen that, at times, project managers are not technically familiar with the respective technologies of the project, making the technical interactions and communication with the development team difficult. However, there are certain things that project managers in this situation can do to work with a development team.

➤ The project manager should address the business logic and provide the developers sufficient freedom for the actual development.

➤ The project manager should resist arguing with the developers on coding techniques. This will only frustrate the developers and have adverse effect on the coding practices.

➤ The project manager should provide the necessary support channels to assist the developers with any technical difficulties they may encounter. One method is to put the developer(s) in touch with other developers who are using similar technologies.

➤ The project manager should offer the developers opportunities to learn the latest IT skills.

## ➤ Prototyping a Solution

Many times a client cannot visualize what the prospective IT system or product will look like until the very end of the project, and this logic leads to changes to the solution, making things complicated for all parties. It is, however, common practice for a project team to develop a prototype or demonstration model of the IT solution early during the design phase.

It may also be the case that the project design team needs to understand the solution, and insist on building a prototype before committing themselves to the project. Prototyping activities usually begin during the (a) requirement or (b) initiation phase and are usually finalized by the end of the design phase.

A prototype is an early exploratory model of the software solution that contains enough capabilities for use in establishing or refining client requirements. It even solves many of the development problems, and by the time the actual development begins, the process is much easier to understand. When developing a prototype model of the proposed system, the project manager must ensure that the prototype reflects the true environment in which the solution will be implemented. The technique used to start the development of the prototype is called rapid application development (RAD). Some of the immediate benefits of prototyping a solution for a client are

➤ Higher acceptance level from the client

➤ Client involvement from day one, thus improving relationships

➤ Restrictions of constant changes downstream (as in a conventional project)

➤ The client becomes familiar through knowledge transfer

## ■ I WISH I HAD KNOWN THAT

There are several precautions that project managers can take to help make sure that the project will reach its fullest potenial. Project managers can keep the schedule up-to-date and make sure it reflects the latest design changes. They should be aware that working with new or unfamiliar technology makes estimation less accurate. They should be sure that the scope of work is very clearly defined and agreed upon before doing the work. There should be clearly defined functionality and quality requirements, as well as agreement about the cost for delivering against these, adjusting as appropriate. If major changes to the project are the result of outside influences (e.g., market changes), then it is essential to review the business case for any change in approach. The following are some useful tips that will help project managers detect early warning signs that a project is unlikely to deliver the business benefits.

➤ Users and project managers do not know (or do not agree on) how every part of the solution will be used to deliver business benefits.

➤ The project sponsor, business managers, or project manager are not clear about mutual responsibility and accountability.

➤ Plans do not include sufficient time to carry out the appropriate business analysis of risk.

➤ No plan exists for accommodating scope change or new requirements.

➤ The scope for the work is incomplete, hence scope – creep, which increases the time and cost of delivering the solution.

➤ New functionality simply does not work, and time and cost increase as effort is expended to make it work.

➤ Insufficient time, money, or resources are allocated to the project.

➤ **Phase Completion Checklist**

The project manager should make sure that the following project documentation is filed within the main project folder in order to complete the project planning phase:

➤ Project definition report or plan

➤ WBS

➤ Project schedule indicating deliverables (GANTT chart)

➤ An activity plan (GANTT chart)

➤ Project charter

➤ Project estimate and budget

➤ Technical specification(s) such as billing or interface specifications

➤ Resource plan and utilization chart

➤ Roles and responsibilities

➤ Status reports

➤ Minutes of the meeting

➤ Any inbound and outbound correspondence

➤ All final project costs, such as timesheets, invoices, and so forth

# Chapter 6

# Executing the Project

## ■ EXECUTING THE PROJECT

The actual execution of any project is an exciting time for all as the execution phase plays an important role. This is where all the previous planning and refinement starts taking shape. This phase clearly indicates that the necessary commitment has been provided to the project in terms of expectations, targets, and schedule. Project managers now need to realize that high quality deliverables will need to be provided from here onwards.

Something that the project manager should be aware of right from the very start of the execution phase of the project is that it is important not only to establish core project meetings with the management team, but also to hold frequent technical meetings with the development team to address the technical progress of the project. If this is not achieved, isolation from certain parties will surely lead to difficulties and communication problems later on.

### ➤ Project Plan Execution

The project manager needs to drive the project plan during the project execution phase. During this process, the project manager continually verifies the scope of the project, monitors the quality of deliverables, and tracks the project resources against the project management plans that have been developed during the planning phase.

## ➤ Developing the Project Team

It is imperative at this stage that all required team members have been assigned to the project and that they have been briefed on the project objectives. The project manager should be aware that part-time or temporary resources on the project have a tendency to be pulled away from the project, either due to other commitments or higher priority assignments. This could prove to be difficult for the project manager as it is highly probable that the project schedule will suffer and it is unlikely that time scales will be met.

## ➤ The Kick-off meeting

This is the stage where the project manager needs to hold a project kick-off the meeting for the group that will be responsible for developing, testing, and supporting the project. In some situations the kick-off meeting may only be held with the development team members who are responsible for designing and developing the solution. Similarly, a separate kick-off meeting is held later on with the implementation team and at the point where the users and client start being involved in the deployment process. The kick-off meeting always tries to bring key members of the respective teams together in order to present the high-level project goals and objectives. The project manager also formally introduces all members and announces their roles on the project during the respective durations.

Prior to the kick-off meeting, the project manager develops a high-level project schedule and plan that identifies the high-level milestones and important events. Copies of this project documentation should be distributed in order to pre-

Project Title

**Project agenda to be held on 08 June at 14:00**
1. Introduction to project team members
2. Project vision and objectives
3. Establishing the client requirements
4. Creating/discussing the project name
5. Identifying the roles and responsibilities per member / team
6. Discussing the project scope and estimated duration
7. Discuss the communication flow on the project
   ➤ Timesheet submission
   ➤ Vacations & time off
   ➤ Overtime
   ➤ Remote working if applicable
   ➤ Dress code on project
   ➤ Rewards and recognition
   ➤ Other
8. Future meetings

Doc No:                                                                  Rev 1.0

**Figure 6.1**    A basic project agenda

pare the expectations of the team members before they en-
ter the kick-off meeting. It is important that the project
manager has arranged for an agenda of items that will be discussed prior to the actual kick-off meeting. Minutes to this
meeting should be documented and distributed to attendees,
within a short period of time, and a copy of the minutes
should be kept in the project folder with all the other project
documentation (see Figure 6.1). The objectives of the kick-
off meeting in the execution phase are

➤ To re-emphasize the aim and objectives of the project

➤ To confirm the scope of the project.

➤ To discuss the approach to the project.

➤ To present the high-level project plan and the current
status of the project

➤ To discuss the roles and responsibilities of each member

➤ To discuss the project communication process

➤ To arrange for the next project meeting

## ➤ Delegating Project Tasks

Team members must know which task or tasks have been assigned to them and they must know when those tasks are to be completed. If members are unaware of this or if the messages are or poorly communicated, the project tasks will end up late or even incorrectly developed. The role of the project manager is to ensure that all parties are comfortable with handling their respective tasks and do not appear confused.

This inability to communicate correctly on a project reminds me of a troubled project that I was told to take charge of. Upon calling the first set of review meetings, I noticed that only senior managers of the various internal departments attended the meetings, as junior members were not required to attend meetings. The meetings proved to be successful and I had felt that I had delegated the project tasks correctly and that these tasks would be carried out. However, as sometimes happens on Fridays, I noticed some of the project members were busy with non-project-related activities, and this concerned me. I had clearly stressed the aspect of working to make up the lost time on the schedule. My immediate discussions with the project developers led me to realize that they were unsure of their tasks to be performed. Three days after I had delegated the tasks, they were still waiting for a full briefing from their managers! I couldn't believe it. Nonetheless, I changed the rules of all future meetings. I started to communicate with and delegate directly to everyone on a daily basis, and I obtained direct feedback in the meetings from each member involved. My meetings were broken up into two separate meetings:

➤ A high-level core meeting where the managers attended and tasks were delegated to them

➤ A technical meeting for the all members in order to communicate responsibilities and make sure that everyone knew what to do

Every project team member should agree that the schedule for his or her tasks is reasonable. Basically, each team member knows his or her role on the project and the extent of his or her authority and responsibility.

Project team members become thoroughly annoyed if they do not know what they are expected to do or when something should be finished. They are also annoyed when they are told to do something that they know they cannot do and are not given adequate opportunity to voice their opinion. The best advice for project managers is to avoid this justified annoyance. You won't regret it. Suffice it to say, communication is the key to a happy, well-run project. An important part of this communication is having a good working relationship with all the team members on the project.

## ■ THE DEVELOPMENT BEGINS

At this stage of the project, the design and development team have provided the most input regarding how long it would take to develop the system and the resources that will be required. A project manager's job is to ensure that the project follows the development time estimates that were provided during the planning phase. It is important that the development team is confident about the activities and deliverables they are expected to meet. A developer may be confident because he or she gave the estimate. On the other hand, a developer may trust the estimation that was given by the technical lead. Either way, a plan works best if individuals commit to performing each task in the timeframe planned. Because project managers have the responsibility of bringing the project to completion in the time specified by the project plan, it is important that they have some degree of confidence in each item of the plan as well. If they are not confident of the individual activities and duration, there is a good chance that poor planning was performed and that the project was not approached correctly.

## ➤ Involvement with Development

The development effort consumes a large amount of resources and takes the biggest chunk out of any project schedule. With it comes many changes and potential for conflict. The project manager should be actively involved during the development, even though the developers on the team will be doing most of the work. This does sound odd, but the project manager needs to keep abreast of the progress of those development tasks. An example of poor project manager involvement with the development team would be where the developers are busy creating an application based upon the project plan, but unbeknownst to the developers, additional changes have been introduced to the design. This most certainly interrupts the entire development process, as the developers may have to restart or redouble their efforts to catch up. The following are some guidelines and tips for the project manager and development team:

➤ The project manager should establish frequent development meetings with team leaders and developers in order to understand any problems developers are facing. This will help determine necessary corrective actions.

➤ The project manger should actively be involved with the development team. It is very important for the project manager to be in tune and pace with the development that is taking place.

➤ The project manger should not change the business logic of the applications developed by the design and development team. A constant change in program logic will disrupt the development process.

➤ The business requirements should be provided to the development team to ensure the correct coding of the applications.

➤ The project manager should frequently assess the current position of the project and see if the development schedule is on track and if the delivery dates can be achieved. If the project is behind schedule, then the project manager should arrange for additional work-hours.

➤ The project manager should foster a knowledge transfer process among developers.

➤ The project manager should meet each developer personally and try to encourage him or her to achieve project objectives.

➤ Team-building activities should be arranged. Taking the team out for lunch may be a good idea.

➤ Placing too much pressure on the developers to rush

and complete the physical development activities will result in errors.

➤ A professional relationship with the development team is encouraged and paves the way for a successful project development. This is achieved by holding frequent communication between all parties. In many cases, developers appreciate recognition for creativity and hard work. This recognition will only boost confidence and give the enthusiasm to work even harder.

➤ If the project demands that the developers work additional hours to meet the project schedule, it is only fitting that the developers receive additional compensation for their work.

➤ A developer's compensation should be competitive with industry standards. In today's marketplace developers will most likely leave the project if they are dissatisfied.

## ■ TESTING ON A PROJECT

When it comes to software projects, it is crucial that testing be performed at certain key points of the project life cycle phases. Certain methodologies, such as the Timeboxing approach, allow for the rapid prototyping and testing at each phase, whereas the more traditional Waterfall approach involves testing only after the development phase has been completed.

At this stage, the project manager must have already notified the testing team of the forthcoming testing. He or she also needs to setup a meeting with the testing and quality assurance (QA) staff. At the test and QA meeting, there will be a series of tasks and responsibilities that the project manager has to communicate to the staff. By default, the following testing staff members can be made available for the testing phase: (1) the developer, (2) the business analyst, (3) the systems analyst, (4) the testers, and (5) the end-user. The project manager must also ensure that necessary staff has been scheduled and is available to perform testing. Any unavailability of resources must be resolved immediately prior to testing beginning.

## ➤ Test Environment

The project manager, together with the testing manager, shall ensure that a suitable testing infrastructure is established and set up prior to any testing taking place. This could imply separate funding for hardware for the project, an additional requirement that should not be overlooked during the planning phase. The necessary software test tools should also be obtained and be available before testing commences. The testing resources should be tested in all the necessary test tools before testing commences. Testing on a project is estimated to cost up to 25 percent of the total budget. The key to any testing effort is creating a suitable test environment in which testing can occur. The project manager should be fully aware that certain test and staging environments will probably be necessary and that these will need to be set up. These test environments involve obtaining and deploying sufficient hardware and software. If this has not been included in the project plan, then it may be too late to compensate for what may be a serious delay on the overall project time line. The testing of any IT project needs to be performed in separate staging environments (see Figure 6.2). They are

➤ The development environment (where development takes place)

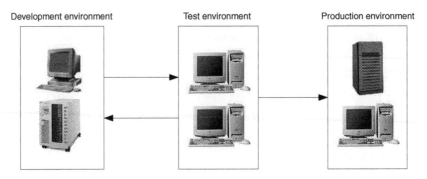

Development environment                    Test environment                    Production environment

**Figure 6.2**   IT staging environments

➤ The test environment (where the solution is tested)

➤ A fully functional production environment (the final location)

Remember that the test environment is the first formal test environment. Characteristics of that environment should include some preparation and planning that are based upon the type of system to be tested. The project manager must include this into the overall planning when the project plan is being created. There are several considerations that need to be taken into account:

➤ An appropriate number of properly configured workstations

➤ Complete network connectivity and communication between components of the system

➤ The correct routers/switches/hubs

➤ File servers

➤ Sufficient disk space to house the application, tools (e.g., editors, debuggers, file compares, query facilities), test data, and test results

➤ Appropriate memory configurations

➤ Simulation of production databases.

➤ Files/tables

# ■ THE IMPORTANCE OF TESTING

Without a well-thought testing effort, the project will undoubtedly fail overall and will impact the entire operational performance of the solution. With a poorly tested solution, the support and maintenance cost will escalate exponentially, and the reliability of the solution will be poor. Therefore, project managers need to realize that the testing effort is a necessity, not merely as an ad hoc task that is the last hurdle before deployment.

The project manager should pay specific attention to developing a complete testing plan and schedule. At this stage, the project manager should have realized that this effort would have to be accommodated within the project budget, as many of the testing resources will be designing, testing, and validating the solution throughout the entire project life cycle—and this consumes work-hours and resources. The testing effort begins at the initial project phase (i.e., preparing test plans) and continues throughout until the closure phase.

## ➤ Testing Criteria

It is essential to conduct tests under realistic conditions. I have often found that testers on a project deliberately go out to destroy the solution during the testing phase in order to do a proper test. Some sensible ground rules for acceptance testing are necessary and need to be established before any testing commences. Typically, some of these rules should include the following:

➤ Using real data and real operators.

➤ Test the solution as the developers build it. This way, errors can be corrected immediately.

➤ Involve project members who understand design and user specifications.

➤ Determine what is included within the test and what is not.

➤ Involve users of the project who know how the system will be used.

➤ Test to see that interfacing the new solution to the current infrastructure has no unexpected consequences.

➤ Allow time for repetition of those unsatisfactory test results in the project schedule.

## ➤ Types of Testing

There are many different types of testing that can take place on an IT project, and the project manager must verify exactly which tests will be required. Table 6.1 presents the most common types of testing that I have encountered, and I have found these to work extremely well.

### Unit Testing

The primary purpose of a unit test is to provide immediate verification that the application code performs as specified at a structural level. Unit test plans are less formal than systems or acceptance test plans. This form of testing may consist of using a simple checklist to perform desk checking, peer reviews, and code walkthroughs. A unit test should examine 100 percent of the processing paths, including edits; it should verify program unit logic, compilation accuracy, data handling capability, interfaces, and design extremes.

**Table 6.1**  Various types of project testing

| Test Types | Tested By | Approach | When is it Performed |
|---|---|---|---|
| Unit testing | Developer | Informal | Continuous during development |
| Integration testing | Developer / QA | Formal | After unit testing "end-to-end" |
| System testing | QA | Formal | Overall testing |
| Pilot testing | Developer | Formal | During Production |
| Performance testing | Sys Admin | Informal | Used to test the speed |
| Stress testing | Developer / Ops | Informal | Used to test the load |
| Functional testing | QA | Formal | After development is completed |
| User acceptance testing (UAT) | User | Formal | After release by QA team |

This is a detailed, low-level test that verifies, among other things, that drop-down lists work, windows can be navigated correctly, toolbars and menus work according to standards, and error messages and help messages work correctly.

The team performs a unit test whenever changes to code are made. In general, the developer who coded the unit executes the tests identified in the unit test plan. Independent testers are not required unless the unit must comply with stringent safety or security requirements. When unit testing is complete, the developer's team leader or application specialist reviews the test results. The reviewer certifies the completeness and correctness of the test (i.e., results are checked against the test plan to ensure that all logic have been tested) and verifies the accuracy of test results. The project manager should be informed of the results and be able to review this with the team. Unit testing is accomplished in the development environment.

### Pilot Testing

With pilot testing, it is necessary that the new system be used by a limited number of production users in their normal production environment. Users should execute functions on the new system, evaluate the results, and assess the impact on performance reliability in their environment. Before a new system is deployed at the user site, a preimplementation pilot test should be performed to simulate the system in the manner for which it will be used. The following guidelines should help the project manager perform preimplementation planning:

➤ The project manager should choose an individual (one who was involved in training and acceptance testing) to be responsible for collating error reports and change requests.

➤ This individual should be given authority to either authorize or make improvements within defined limits.

➤ A process should be established to deal with larger proposals for change.

➤ The project manager should establish a management and reporting structure to monitoring error reports, change requests, and report back to the originators.

➤ The project manager should assess and approve all enhancements and change requests on the basis of their relevance and contribution to the business objectives.

### Functional Testing

The project's quality assurance team is responsible for looking after the functional testing of the solution being developed. It is pretty much front-end, "click and see" type of testing. Functional testing should be designed to ensure that each business specification/requirement has been included and works. The tester or testers shall be responsible for test planning, test documentation, and the validation. I have often found that without proper testing staff on the project team, the project encounters problems. It can even get to the point where the project is delayed due to inconsistencies between the specifications and the system being tested. The project manager must be involved with the test team in order to resolve any possible discrepancies that may exist. An example of this discrepancy would be if the client introduces changes during the project, but these changes were not documented correctly by means of formal change requests. The purpose of functional testing is to detect user interface problems early, before development is nearing final completion and the system is put into production.

### System Testing

A systems test provides functional "end-to-end" verification that the system performs as a complete, integrated product. It's important to mention this type of testing because many projects fail this test. The purpose of system testing is to verify the functionality of the solution in that all requirements and specifications are met. During this test, the test team executes tests specified in the system test plans. Results obtained during test execution are documented, and the development team is notified of any discrepancies. In accordance with stringent configuration management procedures, the developers must correct the discrepancies. The system team retests the corrected software, and regression tests are executed to ensure that previously tested functions have not been adversely affected. The system test plan also defines the set of regression tests that will be used to ensure that changes made to software have had no unintended side effects.

Systems test cases are built on the premise that the developers have completed unit testing. Therefore, the testing team may expect that the code has been compiled correctly and basic functionality is working. This information is provided to the project manager, who then prepares the system for the next step.

System testing begins once unit testing is completed. System tests are planned and executed by the test team, which is a subset of the development team that includes application specialists. The leader of the test team is responsible to the project manager and ensures that test resources are scheduled and coordinated, that the appropriate test environment is established, and that other members of the team understand test tools and procedures to be used. System testing is performed in a separate controlled environment where software and hardware simulate a production environment. A formal configuration management process is also in effect. During testing, the project manager directs the actions of the team, ensures that the test plan is followed, responds to unplanned events, and devises workarounds for failures that threaten the progress of testing. He or she maintains test data and control files under configuration management.

### Integration Testing

Final integration testing is very important to confirming the system's capability. This phase also provides assurance that the new system can be integrated with the other systems and business processes with which it has to work, with no adverse effects on them.

> ➤ A plan for doing all the required tests must be prepared, reviewed, and agreed upon jointly by the purchaser (with the participation of business users of the

systems, IS staff, and purchasing specialists) and the supplier.

➤ The plan, as part of the contract, should specify (1) the individual who has the responsibility and authority for acceptance, (2) other participants, (3) acceptance criteria, and (4) testing procedures.

### Performance or Stress Test

During the life of any IT project, there are times when the project manager must use existing resources (e.g., servers, desktop equipment, etc.), primarily due to budgetary constraints on purchasing new equipment. These resources will have a severe impact on a project if the system performance or volumes cannot be achieved. In order to verify that these resources can perform as required, the team conducts performance, load, and stress testing to determine if there are specific problems that would affect the project. Based on results of this test, tweaking of the system may be necessary. In a worse case scenario, if this tweaking does not work, the project manager must purchase replacement equipment immediately.

### Acceptance Testing

The purpose of the acceptance testing phase is to demonstrate that the system meets requirements in the operational environment. The development team does not perform the acceptance test. Testing is executed to see if the project meets the original client requirements, and it is is only considered complete when all tests specified in the acceptance test plan have been run successfully.

Acceptance testing guarantees compliance with end-user requirements and determines whether a system integrates into the operational environment. Acceptance testing is done after the completion of system testing. At the conclusion of systems testing, there is a meeting to decide if the application is ready for acceptance testing. All known critical defects should be fixed and tested prior to the start of acceptance testing. The goal is to make no more changes to the application or environment once acceptance testing begins.

During acceptance testing, the IT development team assists the test team and may execute the acceptance tests under the direction of the acceptance test team. The development team corrects any errors uncovered by the tests. Acceptance testing is considered complete when all tests specified in the acceptance test plan have been run successfully and the system has been formally accepted. The development team then delivers final versions of the software and system documentation (the user guide and system description) to the customer. The purpose of an acceptance test is to allow the user to verify the following:

➤ The system is stable, works as an integrated system, and is presented to the users as a product.

➤ Databases supporting the system have the scope to cover the business correctly.

➤ Data entry and reports all present data in a correct manner.

➤ The system interacts correctly with existing systems.

➤ Business processes are correctly reflected within the system and allow defined business procedures to operate as required.

➤ Error processing is handled effectively and user help facilities are completed and usable.

➤ System administration functions and system security are correctly supported.

➤ Batch processing within the system and with related systems works within the sequences and timings necessary to support the business.

➤ The system is capable of handling multiple transactions and of supporting concurrent users.

At the end of acceptance testing, when all acceptance tests have been completed, a final report documenting testing results is prepared and maintained in the project folder. This includes a final detailed report on each test, in addition to an overall summary that gives an overview of the testing process and records how many test items passed during each round of testing.

## ➤ Test Cases and Scripts

Test cases are created for the testing effort in order to simulate the products used by the client in a typical day, week, and month of client activity. Subsets of test cases developed for system testing may be used in acceptance testing.

These test scripts should provide information and templates showing how the actual test cases/scripts will be documented. The test cases/scripts document the specific inputs for the test scenarios being used, and their results are required to determine if the transaction is successful or if it results in an error. The format of the test cases/scripts should be developed to allow for the recording of actual results once the test has been run.

For major testing efforts, especially those involving the feeding of test data from one system to another, the progress of test cases should be monitored. In large projects it is common to use an automated test management tool. If an automated tool is not available, a spreadsheet should be created to track the progress of test cases. The current status on all defects should be made available and be updated at regular test meetings.

# ■ PROJECT BUDGET

Once the project manager has been assigned to the project, it is very likely he or she will learn how important funding and cash flow are to an organization for those projects that have approved funding. Certain organizations require that the allocated project funds be spent before their financial year is complete, as these funds cannot be rolled over to the following financial year. The remaining organizations do not follow this process and allow for financial rollovers. When working with the budget, the project manager needs to determine which plan the company is using. The project manager needs to process the necessary equipment lists and resources and put them into the financial process. By this stage, the project budget is fixed and the project's success is measured against the cash flow and also meeting the budget. It's no use having the budget but waiting until the end to try to spend it.

## ➤ Working with the Budget

Once in the execution phase, the project budget should already form the baseline for which all project costs are measured. From this point forward, it becomes extremely difficult to turn back. The project manager should understand that the budget is fixed and that no additional funds will be allocated to the project. However, many projects do not follow this route, as many organizations or even their own departments have phenomenal budgets, and can allow for the transfer or re-allocation of funds from one account to assist the ailing project budget. In such environments, project managers simply advocate for additional funding when needed.

| Cash Flow Schedule | | | | | | | | |
|---|---|---|---|---|---|---|---|---|
| ID Resource Type | Jan | Feb | Mar | Apr | May | Jun | Jul |
| 1   Labor | $5,000 | $6,000 | $5,000 | $3,000 | $7,000 | $4,000 | $2,000 |
| 2   Suppliers | $9,000 | $2,000 | $0 | $8,000 | $0 | $4,000 | $1,000 |
| 3   Equipment | $1,000 | $25,000 | $5,000 | $15,000 | $0 | $0 | $0 |
| 4   Stationary | $300 | $0 | $600 | $0 | $500 | $80 | $0 |
| 5   Travel | $800 | $1,000 | $0 | $5,000 | $5,000 | $0 | $400 |
| 6   Total Monthly Cost | $16,000 | $34,000 | $10,600 | $31,000 | $12,500 | $8,080 | $3,400 |

**Figure 6.3**   Managing the project cash flow

A successful project manager is instrumental in managing the project budget at all times, and he or she must ensure that actual expenses are in line with the initial estimates and planning. As the project is being executed, those planned resource expenses such as computer hardware or software should be ordered and paid for out of the project budget, not general company budgets. The goal is for the project manager to manage the budget and projected cash flow almost as if he or she were managing his or her own business. Managing the budget allows the project manager to be sensitive to overspending and exceeding costs (see Figure 6.3). Strong fiscal discipline will pave the way to project success. It is common for many organizations that deliver solutions to award their project managers lucrative incentives for achieving project success and repeat business from their clients.

## ➤ Ensuring Financial Support for the Project

During the life of the project, it is very likely that the client's or supplier's financial department will contact the project manager regarding certain financial matters. This could be to inquire or to request information from the project manager regarding

➤ Resource rates and bonuses allocated to project staff

➤ Overtime payments

➤ New resources hired on the project

➤ Cash flow projections

➤ Outstanding payments and purchase order documentation

➤ Approval of contractor invoices

➤ Items that are over budget

➤ Project work in progress

It becomes crucial for the project manager to understand the role of the financial department and the importance it plays as a support function for the project. Some financial support tasks could take considerable time to expedite and to be put into motion, and it therefore becomes necessary to know the time it takes to process. This alone will solve many of the project manager's frustrations.

## ■ PROCUREMENT OF EQUIPMENT AND SERVICES

In today's vast technological landscape, it is highly unlikely that one single company will be able to supply its own products and services for an IT solution. Some of these products or services will have to be obtained from external sources, and as such, the project manager will end up having to manage the entire process of negotiating and procuring these resources once the project is executed.

The project manager must review, negotiate, and approve all supplier and subcontractor project delivery dates and schedules in order to map them against the master project plan. The project manager is also the single point of contact for authorizing work during the execution phase. This includes conducting formal project reviews, performing ongoing risk assessments, and controlling supplier and subcontractor activities.

### ➤ Maintaining Contractual Documentation

All contractual documentation that is related to the project or solution should be formally identified once received and be kept under formal documentation management. Some examples of contractual documentation include a (1) client contract, (2) purchase order, (3) letter of intent, (4) official client correspondence, and even (5) minutes of a meeting stating contractual terms and agreements. To maintain contractual documentation, the project manager should create a formal project folder for all contractual documentation and file papers in the order that they are received from the client or suppliers. This folder should be controlled by the financial department, the configuration and documentation department of the company, or the project office.

## ■ CONFIGURATION MANAGEMENT

All projects depend upon good configuration management, and the project manager needs to understand that change will take place during the project life cycle. This change needs to be managed. Configuration management is the term applied to where all the project information (including source code, documentation, content, and systems) is correctly identified, controlled, and maintained for possible future use. It is advisable that the project manager develops a configuration management process for tracking any change requests. Configuration management has four prime areas of interest:

1. *Configuration identification.* This area is concerned with being able to identify all items on a project that must be placed under control.

2. *Configuration change control.* A process is established where the project manager can track all change requests on the project and can assess the impact of these changes to the project schedule and resources.

3. *Configuration accounting.* This area is concerned with being able to draw the necessary configuration reports on the project and account for all configuration items on the project.

4. *Configuration auditing.* This area is concerned with being able to assess and audit the project from a configuration perspective. The outcome of the audit will allow the project manager to implement the necessary corrective actions.

## ➤ Managing Scope Creep

To any seasoned project manager, the thought of implementing the solution as designed is the perfect scenario. However, it is likely that before implementing a new system, a flow of change requests for modifications and enhancements will start pouring in from various sources. This should make the project manager consider carefully the decisions at hand.

There may already be a backlog of changes that were requested, but not incorporated, during the systems development process. Initially, there will be many requests for small improvements and some customization. However, these will be followed by requirements for major changes as the needs of the business change. Inevitably, as a project develops, new requirements and system capabilities are discovered. A well-planned project should be able to take advantage of these, but only if the changes are judged relevant to the core business objectives and they do not increase the risks involved in the project.

## ■ I WISH I HAD KNOWN THAT

The following are some guidelines to help project managers during the execution phase.

➤ Some project methodologies are not the same and may require different development processes.

➤ Data quality and project consistency can be major stumbling blocks in achieving success.

➤ Make sure that all the tools are in place for the staff.

➤ Monitor project costs and time in order to avoid overruns.

➤ Keep project meetings on a frequent basis and communicate status to all stakeholders. Often, project managers get so caught up with project issues that they neglect communication issues, which can cause some conflict later on. A project manager who does not communicate effectively could hear, "We were not informed as to the urgency this task, so we left it 'till later,"or, "You did not tell us we could do that."

➤ If you don't have the necessary resources and available time to perform testing on the project, you are lost!

➤ Early test preparation leads to the resources understanding what to do and uncovers possible problems.

➤ Ensure the testers stress the limitations of the solution.

➤ Tests must be planned by the testers and be synchronized with the overall project schedule.

➤ Ensure that the business requirements and project
plan are updated to the stage that the testing begins.
Incomplete or outdated documentation delays the
testing process!

➤ Review all testing reports. Verify and discuss with the
development team the corrections to be reworked and
the impact they could have on the timeline.

## ➤ Phase Completion Checklist

The project manager should ensure that the following project documentation is filed within the main project folder in
order to complete the project execution phase:

➤ Updated project plan

➤ Updated project schedule

➤ Quality assurance plan

➤ Test plan with relevant test cases

➤ Contingency plan

➤ Status reports

➤ Minutes of the meeting

➤ Any inbound and outbound correspondence

➤ All final project costs, such as timesheets, invoices,
and so forth

# Chapter 7

# Controlling the Project

## ■ PROJECT CONTROL AND MONITORING

If I were to define what the control phase of a project was, I would begin by stating that the project manager must continually measure and control all variances throughout all phases of a project life cycle. You can equate control of a project with the navigation of a sailing boat. It is the captain's responsibility that the vessel remains on its predetermined plotted course and that it reaches its final destination. Similarly, the project manager needs to keep the project on the course set by its plotted objectives.

An accurate snapshot of the actual project (where it is) and with the planned status (where it is supposed to be) must be made at regular intervals, as this is the only way to control a project.

The aim of project control, in a nutshell, is to compare the actual progress and performance against the project plan. The project manager therefore has to analyze any variances, review possible alternatives, and take the appropriate corrective action. Undoubtedly, project managers need to control their projects on a regular basis; without this control being in place, an ever-increasing level of unnecessary detail will appear. Table 7.1 illustrates the key differences between monitoring and corrective actions.

**Table 7.1**  Monitoring and related corrective actions on a project

| Monitoring | Corrective Action |
| --- | --- |
| Measuring progress | Determining the corrective actions needed |
| Comparing actual results to planned results | Assessing performance and improvement |
| Evaluating gaps on the project | Updating changes to the required plans |
| Predicting possible outcomes and trends | Communicating and adjusting total project plan |

Without effective control and preventative measures in place, the project manager is not able to determine which milestones or tasks are behind schedule, over budget, what the issues or risks are, or even by how far the project is failing. I have found that the longer a project is left uncontrolled, the more difficult it becomes to anticipate what problems the project will encounter. The project manager's prime role during this phase is to (a) identify all symptoms or factors that would jeopardize the project and (b) outline the process for bringing the project back on track.

This chapter helps project managers understand those issues and factors that they need to control on any project. It is my goal that readers will be in full control or understand the control techniques for their projects by the time they complete this chapter.

Because projects are large efforts that involve many variables, unexpected things happen from time to time, and these do affect the project. A seasoned project manager allows for minor setbacks, whereas major setbacks (such as missing a major milestone or critical task) necessitate that the project manager take emergency countermeasures and immediately work on the issues and risks. In some cases, it may be too late and will cause the project to fall behind schedule or exceed the allocated costs for that item. To bring a project on schedule and on budget, project managers must know, at all times, how the project is progressing and what is causing any slippages. Company executives require project managers to be able to control their projects and, as such, require constant project progress reports. A project manager can control the project using a basic, three-step process.

1. Determine project status and if objectives are being met.

2. Compare the status against project planning.

3. Assess the cause of problems and implement corrective actions.

## ➤ What the Project Manager Controls

The project manager has to measure many things during the course of a project, and he or she must take actions to guarantee that control (see Figure 7.1). The project manager must

➤ Measure and review the project schedule progress against the plan

➤ Measure and review the project cost progress against the plan

➤ Measure and review project quality

➤ Anticipate possible changes and alternatives

➤ Manage issues and risks

➤ Control scope creep through a change management process

➤ Ensure that delivery of milestones takes place according to client expectations

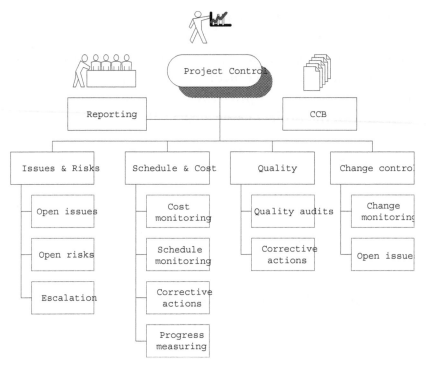

**Figure 7.1** Elements of project control

➤ Coordinate the project team

➤ Monitor physical resources by controlling the scheduling of resources during the project

➤ Communicate project status to the team

## ■ KEY CONTROL AREAS

### ➤ Controlling the Project Schedule

There are several ways to update the schedule. The most frequently used methods are percent completed, remaining duration, duration completed, estimated completion date, and actual start and actual finish dates. The goal is to provide enough information to compare accurately the present project status to the planned target.

Project managers should always be aware that any delay in project implementation places the project at risk of possibly being overtaken by technological change. If this is the case, it is vital that project plans are flexible enough to allow for the insertion of newer technologies when they are released. Some of the schedule issues that need to be controlled are

➤ Erroneous activity sequencing (incorrect WBS)

➤ Project tasks being incorrect because the quantities of resources are unavailable

➤ Changing requirements (which always require additional rework and time)

➤ Incorrect or unrealistic activity duration estimates

## ➤ Controlling Project Resources

The responsibility of managing the correct quantity of resources on a project is demanding. Project managers must ensure that sufficient resources are used on all project activities that were planned earlier during the project-planning phase. In many situations, there are either too little or too many staff members performing these tasks, and it becomes the responsibility of the project manager to level these resources out and to maintain the right amount of resources on the task. It doesn't make any financial sense to keep additional resources on the project if they won't be used again. So, these members will likely have to be released. If the resources have specialist skills that are considered crucial to the client, then the necessary arrangements must be made to retain those resources.

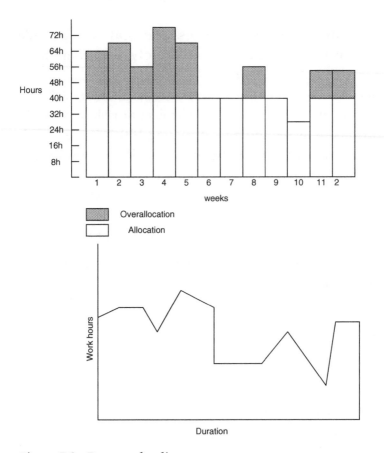

**Figure 7.2** Resource leveling

If, however, project managers find that they have too few resources working on an important task that has to be completed within a certain date, then there are a few options available (see Figure 7.2).

➤ Add additional staff members from other tasks to the important task, hoping to reduce the duration.

➤ Hire additional resources just for the task duration.

## ➤ Controlling Project Costs

The project manager must capture, track, and control all project-related costs that are incurred against planned project cost items. Whether it is project timesheets, hardware, or travel expenses, it is essential that all costs be reflected against the project. This provides a realistic measure of what the project cost the company at the end of the day. Additionally, it also helps measure how well the project was planned.

It is necessary that these costs be captured on the project system that the project manager is using. In the event where unforeseen costs arise, it is the project manager's responsibility to immediately compare the cost item (invoice) against the planned project cost WBS task. If there is a difference, it implies a loss on the specific WBS work package, not necessarily on the total project. If the tendency is similar on many of the WBS tasks, then it is probable that the project will be heading for a loss, indicating bad planning and estimation. There is nothing that the project manager is able to do. To aid the project managers in cost control, the following items need to be verified:

➤ The budget allocations are accurate and correct.

➤ The original project estimate and budget are correct.

➤ The original prices used to develop the estimate still apply and are firm.

➤ Technical difficulties will affect the cost of the project.

However, when costs are incurred against the project and it is found that an actual cost item is slightly higher than the planned WBS cost, the project manager must ensure that, for the project to remain profitable to the company, no more additional cost overruns can be tolerated. The costs must now be controlled even more than ever. Remember, depending on the contract value, the overall project will not immediately reflect this loss; initially only single WBS items reflect this loss. The project manager needs to communicate this necessary information to the executive team. Let's assume the following project scenario:

> As project manager you planned the project extremely well, received the purchase order from the client, and commenced work on a $400,000 IT project. During your initial estimations and planning you obtained quotations from your hardware vendor for $60,000. Subsequently, you included your company markup on the hardware and came to a WBS cost item of $65,000. However, during the project, the vendor informs you of manufacturer increases, and the vendor's new cost is now $66,000. You immediately review the WBS, and it reflects a shortfall of – $1,000. Not only have you failed to break even, you realize you are over budget for this item. You explore alternative vendors, but none exist. Accordingly, you inform the executive team of the cost overrun and the decision is made to carry the cost. The project manager does not want the project to run into similar financial losses and realizes that if the remaining project costs (schedule and travel) are kept in check and even improved, the possibility exists to reduce the shortfall and still maintain the profit margin.

# ■ ADDRESSING EARNED VALUE

I'll be honest and state that I never formally attended an earned value (EV) course, as most of my time was engulfed on physical projects, and it took me a long time to understand what the concept of earned value was all about. In my search to learn something on earned value, I found out that being directly exposed to projects where I dealt with project costs and reporting helped me understand it better. Sure, there are some basic EV formulas to learn, and one needs to apply the concept a few times to get it right. However, once someone has the hang of it, it will put a new perspective on the way that person looks at any project in the future, and this makes it such an exciting tool to use.

There are those groups that advocate that earned value is extremely complex to implement within an organization and that it is seen as a way to circumvent already established financial processes that are currently used within organizations. But this is not the case: Project managers also need to have the necessary tools and abilities to monitor and report accurately on their project performance at a moment's notice. Earned value offers this ability.

Simply put, earned value is a project technique that project managers can use to monitor, track, and report on the performance of any project. Its use is not limited just to the super projects, as it applies equally to both small and medium sized projects. The technique lends itself to jointly plotting both the project schedule and cost values on an S-curve chart or table. Once used, the project manager can very quickly highlight positive or negative variances. The project manager cannot just measure the project schedule alone and make the assumption that project tasks are ahead of schedule and that the project is doing well. It may very well be the case that the project is exceeding project costs, making it unprofitable. This is why both schedule and cost have to be measured simultaneously to gain a more accurate picture (see Figure 7.3).

## ➤ Cost and Schedule Variance

Project managers have traditionally always measured the actual project costs to their planned costs as documented in

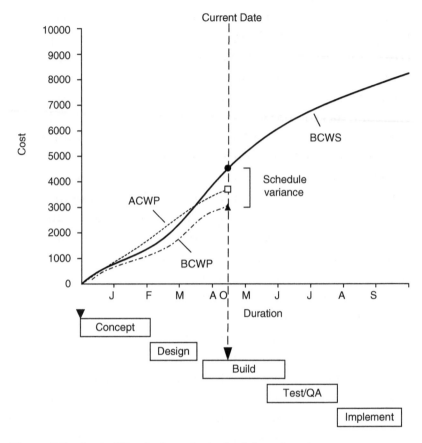

**Figure 7.3**  Controlling both project schedule and cost

their project plans and budgets. There are a few possible variances a project manager could face.

1. *Positive cost variance.* This indicates that the project manager is well within spending and is under budget for project tasks or activities. For example, Task G had $6,000 planned against it, but only $4,800 was spent on this task. This indicates a positive variance of $1,200.

**2.** *Negative cost variance.* This indicates that there is a cost overrun on the project and that it is over budget for specific project tasks or activities. This is basically a red flag for the project manager. For example, Task D had $9,000 planned against it, but the project manager actually spent $9,600 on this task. This indicates a negative variance of –$600.

The previously mentioned cost variances, unfortunately, do not take anything relating to the project schedule into account, and that's our problem. We have to rely on earned value to supplement our example in terms of schedule as well. Let's re-examine the cost variance scenarios again.

Here we subtract our actual costs (actual cost of work performed, or ACWP) from our earned value (budgeted cost of work performed, or BCWP) to get our results. So, if Task G had $6,000 planned against it and had actual costs of **ACWP = $4,800** and we assume we have earned a **BCWP calculation of = $5,000,** then the cost variance (CV) for Task G is **BCWP – ACWP,** which is **$5,000 – $4,800 = $200.** This indicates a positive cost variance of $200 and can be also seen as a cost saving of $200.

Similarly, let's examine our other example. Task D had $9,000 planned against it and has actual costs of **ACWP = $9,600.** If we assume we have earned a **BCWP calculation of $8,000** then the CV for Task D is **BCWP – ACWP,** which is **$8,000 – $9,600 = –$1,600.** This indicates a negative cost variance of –$1,600 and can also be seen as a cost overrun on the project.

The EV technique obviously blows a lot of traditional techniques out of the water, in that project managers previously only monitored their Gantt charts or separate cost reports generated from financial systems. Using earned value,

**Table 7.2**  Earned value formulae

| Earned Value | Determines |
|---|---|
| Budgeted cost of work scheduled (BCWS) | A project manager uses BCWS to represent the value of work to be budgeted. |
| Actual cost of work performed (ACWP) | A project manager uses ACWP to represent the actual cost spent to complete the task. |
| Budgeted cost of work performed (BCWP) | This is also known as earned value. |
| Cost variance (CV) | This is known as the difference between the planned and actual costs for the completed tasks. It can either be positive or negative in value. |
| Cost variance percentage (CV%) | This is expressed as a percentage. A positive value is good: It means the project is under budget. However, a negative value means that the project is over budget, and that is cause for immediate correction. |
| Estimate at completion (EAC) | This is used to recalculate a project budget, in order to obtain a more accurate value of what the project will cost at the end. |

project managers are able to simultaneously monitor and control both schedule and cost using the set of formulae shown in Table 7.2.

Because many clients have their financial departments prepare financial reports and monitor work in progress, either at a project or operational level, these financial reports are generated either at quarterly or monthly. This is accordingly far too late to control project costs and any identified problems, which, in turn, would often be to late for any corrective action to take place. The project manager, on the other hand, cannot wait that long to control his or her project costs and therefore needs to be proactive in much shorter intervals — often on a daily or weekly basis. It is recommended that

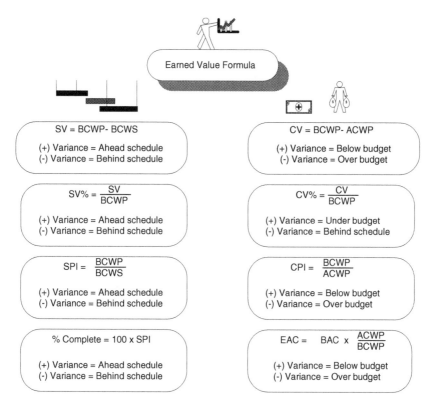

**Figure 7.4**   Earned value formulae

projects be controlled from the 15 percent mark. There is no doubt that earned value, if properly applied, is highly effective in giving a meaningful measure of progress. And, the principles are just as valid for IT development managers as they are for project managers (see Figure 7.4).

## ➤ The 50-50 and 0-100 Rules

Many project managers traditionally report project schedule progress by using an incremental estimation method. This method normally starts by estimating tasks at levels such as 15 percent, 40 percent, 78 percent, or 98 percent, incrementally moving forward until 100 percent complete.

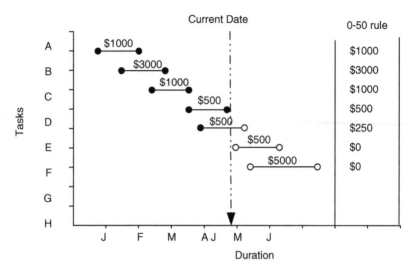

**Figure 7.5** The 50-50 rule technique

This process is based on no proper quantitative measurement and is often inaccurate. Additionally, this information is, in turn, submitted to either the project office or executives to review, and perceptions at the senior level are based on inaccurate project data.

Project managers could possibly consider adopting a more accurate method of reporting on project progress. In the project world, two of these methods are the 50-50 and 0-100 rules. However, in the IT environment, the 50-50 rule is more commonly used. The important thing to remember is to keep it simple (see Figure 7.5). Remember that keeping the schedule variance simple on the progress reporting side makes calculating the EV easier to manage. The way to implement the 50-50 rule is fairly straightforward.

➤ Assign 50 percent of the BCWP to the task the moment the task is started. At this point it is assumed that half the work has been done already.

➤ Assign 100 percent of the BCWP the moment the task ends. This is only allocated once the task actually finishes.

The 0-100 rule works exactly the same way:

➤ Assign 0 percent to indicate that the project task has not yet begun.

➤ Assign 50 percent to indicate that the task is halfway complete.

➤ Assign 100 percent to indicate that the project is complete.

## ➤ Maintaining the Cost Baseline

It is important to establish a project baseline, as this is necessary to measure the actual values incurred at any time on the project against the planned values. Project managers should realize that they have to measure their progress against the baseline plan during all the subsequent project phases and that the level of tracking increases exponentially during a deployment project. Project managers should establish a review strategy and communication plan to encourage current, accurate, and consistent feedback.

## ➤ Time Sheets

All projects, in some or another, utilize time sheets as the foundation for capturing and coordinating work performed on the project. Timesheets are simple in principle and have the advantage of offering information that comes directly from the people who are actually doing the project tasks.

Timesheets are useful to any project and should be submitted by team members on a (1) weekly, (2) semi-monthly, or a (3) monthly basis. These time sheets indicate the project tasks that resources are working on (e.g., John worked 180 hours on WBS item 20.4.3 for the month of July) and are authorized either by the project manager or client. The timesheets are consolidated and used accordingly for billing or invoicing purposes. If timesheets are an important part of the invoicing cycle, the project managers must be made aware of the anticipated cash flow at each month by the contracting team. Late or delayed timesheets affect this cash flow and also affect the company's financial position. The project manager should also consolidate the hours worked per WBS item and capture these work-hours against the budgeted planned hours. Today, many project software tools allow for timesheet capturing.

## ➤ Daily Project Activities Checklist

A vital part of any project manager's responsibilities is to take charge of the day-to-day activities on the project. These include monitoring the progress of project tasks and activities and making decisions about the project. Most importantly, these tasks and activities should be managed on a daily or weekly basis.

The best way to gather this project information is to ask the project team members how their tasks are progressing. Project managers have come to understand that nothing substitutes for actually asking team members, face to face, how their part of the project is going. Project managers are much more likely to get a true picture of the facts. They then incorporate and update this progress information into the respective project documentation. Table 7.3 shows which documentation needs to be controlled on a regular basis.

Remember that the project executives rely on the project manager's status reports and communications when they are reviewing and making important strategic decisions. If

**Table 7.3**   Frequency checklist

| What | How to Update | Frequency |
| --- | --- | --- |
| Project definition report or plan | Update existing documents | As needed |
| The weekly project status report | Issue new status report | Weekly |
| Daily issue and risk log | Update issue or risk log | Daily |
| Computerized tracking tools | Review and track | Daily |
| Change request forms | Submit changes to change control board (CCB) | As needed |

these documents show that a project is behind schedule or over budget, then it fuels the question as to whether executives need to cancel the project entirely or see it through to the end, as it is strategically important from a business perspective. Nonetheless, the project manager is the person accountable for reporting the accurate and true status of the project at frequent intervals (see Figure 7.6). I have personally found that submitting status reports on a weekly basis works best.

# ■ CONTROLLING PROJECT RISK

Risk control is the process of continually assessing the condition of the project and developing options to permit alternative solutions (see Figure 7.7). Project managers should take care to identify consequences that are likely to occur and any indicators of the start of the problem. The following are some suggestions for risk control:

➤ Continually update the risk management plan.

➤ Implement risk avoidance actions.

➤ Implement risk contingency actions.

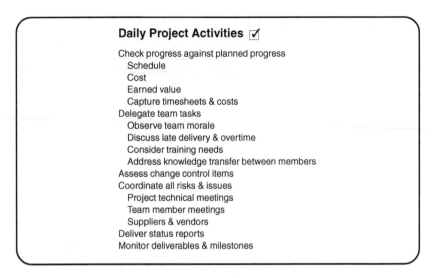

**Figure 7.6**   Daily project activity checklist

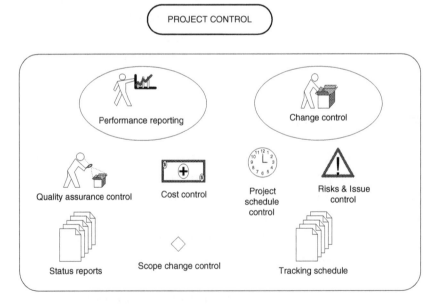

**Figure 7.7**   Control issues to monitor

➤ Report on each risk issue.

➤ Monitor and analyze the effectiveness.

## ➤ Updating the Project Risk Log

Risk quantification involves the process of evaluating risks and determining the effect the risk will have on your project. One of the easiest ways to determine risk quantification of project risks is to multiply the potential impact (I) of the risk's occurrence with the probability (P) of it occurring. The probability of occurrence is the degree of belief that various events will occur. The potential severity of impact is the significance of the event if it happens. Once quantified, each risk needs to be prioritized by the project manager onto a risk matrix. This action ensures that efforts are focused on only the most significant ones. The formula commonly used is

$$R = I \times P$$
**Risk (%) = Impact × Probability**

**I** = Assign a value between (1–10) the impact it will have.
**P** = Assign a value between (1–10) the probability of it occurring.

Once the value(s) have been determined, the project manager allocates a percentage (%) to the risk, and this then allows him or her to categorize and prioritize the identified risk. Table 7.4 gives an example of a risk and issue matrix. The risk (%) is tabled as follows:

> 80 = Priority One

> 50 – 79 = Priority Two

> 30 – 49 = Priority Three

< 30 = Priority Four

**Table 7.4** Risk and issue matrix

| ID | Project Area | Description of Risk | I | P | Score | Solution |
|----|----|----|----|----|----|----|
| 1 | Client | Need URS signed off—ver 1.0 | 9 | 9 | 81 | Begin negotiations |
| 2 | CCB | New change request—new database | 7 | 7 | 49 | Review change req. |
| 3 | Design | Hardware spec to be finalized | 6 | 5 | 30 | Finalize by 10/1 |

The risk matrix primarily works extremely well and lets project managers proactively document and resolve all identified issues and risks made during the project life cycle. As the project continues, risks identified early on in the planning phase will be resolved and the eventuality of new ones being raised during the later phases is good. Project managers need to be prepared for risks and the difficulty and rate at which they surface. Each risk needs to be documented, irrespective of the rating it is given.

The risk matrix should form the basis of a working project document, and it needs to be formally communicated to all project stakeholders in order for these stakeholders to obtain a current perspective on the project. I once observed a project manager trying his very best to resolve project risks in total isolation, and this led to communication problems and the eventual cancellation of the project by executives — all because they could not see a visible project leader and had no assurance as to the project being in control.

## ➤ Identifying Issues

It is necessary that project managers identify issues as quickly as possible in order that they be addressed and resolved. Items that do surface during the project life cycle that require follow-up must be captured in an Issue Log and be resolved quickly. In order to identify any project issues, it is also important that the project manager knows which questions to ask during the course of project meetings and reviews. The problem is that when working on a project, the people who are to provide the answers are not always available to do so, so the project manager needs to take the lead and do whatever it takes to get the necessary answers.

# ■ PROJECT CHANGE CONTROL

Change can be generated by anyone, but this is not to say that the required change will be actually implemented on a project. Changes to a project may be a result of a (1) deviation or waiver, (2) issue management process, or (3) a change in scope as requested by the client. If a deviation is identified from the agreed-upon assumptions and constraints, or if the client is unwilling to meet their obligations, a change in the project or the project targets may result. Resolving an issue may mean changing the way the project is being approached or changing scope. In many cases, there may be a clear modification to scope wherein the client requests additional functionality or deliverables, or perhaps even a reduction in functionality or deliverables.

Developers and designers sometimes introduce technical "requirements" to a project that do not actually contribute to the business success of the project. Essentially, no matter how "nice" something is, it should not be done unless there is a clear business benefit that is within the scope of the project.

Project managers should at least be aware of new requirements before they are implemented. Many projects suffer from users, business analysts, and even technical architects wandering from developer to developer and inserting "good ideas" into the project. While this is done with

**Table 7.5**  Change control tracking list

| ID | Description of Change Request | Submission Date | Schedule Impact | Cost Impact | Status |
|---|---|---|---|---|---|
| 1 | Change web UI pick list | 9/29/01 | 4 days | $7,000 | Approved |
| 2 | Modify month end report | 03/24/02 | 2 weeks | $6,000 | Approved |
| 3 | Migrate data to new platform | 10/20/01 | 2 months | $80,000 | Cancelled |
| 4 | Include search engine XYZ | 10/28/01 | 1 month | $14,000 | Pending |
| | **Net Project Impact (Approved Change Requests)** | | | $13,000 | |

the best of intentions, it has a terrible impact on the schedule and must be controlled. This is not to say that all "techie" tasks should be dismissed out of hand; however, things that are necessary should be sold to the business on the basis of benefit to the business, and they should be included in the business requirements for the project. Table 7.5 illustrates a change control tracking spreadsheet that lists all the change requests approved on the project. The schedule and cost effect can also be taken into account.

## ➤ Change Control: A Process

It is important to control the change requests that are proposed during the course of the project. The following step-by-step process will help project managers implement successful change control.

1. Initiate scope change requests by completing a scope change request form.

2. Track scope change requests by logging them in a scope change control log.

3. Determine how the scope change will be identified and prioritized.

4. Assess the impact; examine the tasks, schedule, cost, and quality affected by the scope change.

5. Select the recommended solution to the scope change.

6. Meet with the owner to accept or reject the change.

7. Implement the scope changes order, if required, and document the changes.

8. Communicate to the project team so all members understand the affect of the scope change.

## ➤ Changes to the Project Scope

Change management ensures the smooth integration of the existing (production) code and operating system with any planned introduction of an alteration, variance, or improvement. The change management process is invoked whenever changes are being introduced into the targeted environment.

## ➤ Dealing with Version Control

Once approved, all project documentation and plans should be referred to as the baseline plan. Remember that plans are often revised and it is common for project members to work with different or outdated documents or plans. Therefore, all plans should be managed and placed under strict configuration management. The project manager's prime directive is to ensure that all changes made to project documentation are captured correctly and approved accordingly. The documentation should also reflect the appropriate version number, date, and an index of all changes made to the respective document before it is distributed to project members.

## ➤ Tracking Changes

There are many configuration management tools on the market that richly deserve credit for their ability to track changes to both software and to the development process. Some are more complex than others and offer incredible perspectives on the changes about to be made to systems. Project Managers need to track all proposed changes to the project on an ongoing basis.

## ➤ Change Control Board Responsibilities

Any anticipated changes to a project need to be reviewed from a technical and business perspective before any proposed change can take effect. The change control board (commonly know as "CCB") consists of a chairperson and technical and business members who appoint subject matter experts on an "as-needed" basis. They meet on a frequent basis to review the change requests or when requested by the project manager.

Very often at large organizations, it is common to find a dedicated CCB in place, serving all change requests within the project and operational environment. In this case, the project manager needs to determine the process of functions within the CCB. The CCB can perform the following:

➤ Approve change requests made to the project

➤ Reject the change request

➤ Defer the change request until further assessments or recommendations are made

Normally, an average-sized project cannot afford the manpower and the time to develop these change processes from scratch, so it is often left to the project manager to form his or her own CCB, often involving the client in the process.

## ➤ Controlling Conflict on the Project

On almost every project, the potential for conflict arises at some point. This is a natural trend. The project manager should work proactively with all staff to avoid possible conflicts that may arise. In the event of a conflict, the project manager should be aware that talking can only resolve so much. For situations where conflict cannot be resolved through negotiations or arbitration, it is recommended that the identified individuals be separated or be removed from the project.

It is important to understand that project staff react differently to daily situations and that during the project life cycle, these members all experience various emotions such as joy, sadness, jealousy, anger, frustration, and stress — to name but a few. Many conflicts can be reduced or eliminated by constantly communicating the project objectives to the project team members. Some of the most common conflicts are

- ➤ Conflict over project priorities
- ➤ Conflict over administrative procedures
- ➤ Personality conflicts
- ➤ Lack of respect for one another
- ➤ Conflict over technical opinions and performance
- ➤ Conflict over staffpower resources
- ➤ Conflict over cost
- ➤ Conflict over schedules

When conflicts do arise, there are several methods to try to resolve them.

1. *Compromise.* Parties consent to agree; each side wins or loses a few points.

2. *Confrontation.* Parties work together to find a solution to the problem.

3. *Forcing.* Power is used to direct the solution. One side gets what the other does not.

4. *Smoothing.* This technique plays down the differences between two groups and gives strong attention to the points of agreement.

5. *Withdrawal.* This technique involves one party removing him- or herself from the conflict.

# ■ MANAGING QUALITY

For the project manager, quality management is all about ensuring that everything that is done or produced fits the purpose for which it is being done or produced. There are two main facets to quality management: (1) quality assurance (QA) and (2) quality control. In order to perform testing effectively in a software development effort, the QA manager needs to determine ways to show progression and improvement of the process and of the deliverable product. Measuring the effectiveness of testing serves the following purposes:

➤ Evaluates the performance of testing to uncover defects

➤ Quantifies the quality of the program/application process

➤ Provides a confidence factor to predict potential occurrences of errors once the system is released

➤ Provides data for potential improvement opportunities

➤ Justifies the expenses of the unit/resources to contribute to the end product's usefulness

The postimplementation review process provides a structure for identifying opportunities for continual improvement. It assesses the results of a release or of an entire system. The QA manager is often responsible for developing indicators for the review. The intent is to develop a picture of what was successful in the process of development and testing and what might be improved. Indicators are agreed upon in advance during system development and are documented in a template.

## ➤ Updating Project Documentation

It is important that, throughout the project's life cycle, project managers update and distribute all new approved changes to the existing project documentation in order to reflect any changes to the project plans or schedule. A distribution list developed during the initiation phase should detail the recipients, communication methods, and number of copies required.

## ➤ Conducting Quality Inspections

Project managers should obtain feedback from the project owner, stakeholders, or both to determine that their quality requirements are being met. He or she should make sure that the project team members report compliance or noncompliance to the quality plan, specifications, and procedures. Throughout the project's life cycle, the project manager should generate reports that are related to quality issues and performance, as well as perform periodic quality audits. He or she should record lessons learned that address any quality issues or problems encountered in the project and the associated resolutions.

## ➤ Quality Assurance

QA involves all planning, design, work, and procedures necessary to ensure that quality is achieved—in other words, to ensure that what is done or produced is fit for its purpose. Hence, QA can be thought of as activity that takes place before any work is done.

## ➤ Quality Control

Quality control is the inspection of finished products to ensure that they meet required standards or are fit for their purpose. Where products fail, remedial action is taken. Thus,

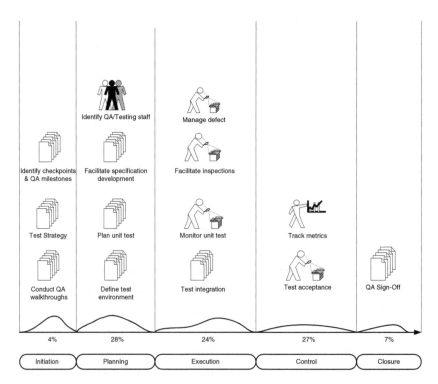

**Figure 7.8** Quality assurance and control

quality control is normally considered something that goes on after the work has been done. It makes no sense at all to keep on doing things wrong in the hope that mistakes will be picked up and rectified in quality control.

## ➤ Project Status Reporting

Throughout all individual phases of the project, the project manager is required to develop and distribute regular project status reports to key stakeholders who are involved with the project. Remember that status reports keep everyone informed of the current status of the project and the progress being made. This report also highlights any unresolved issues or action items. Items that are part of project status reporting include

➤ Executive high-level project schedules

➤ Periodic status reports

➤ Weekly status reports

➤ Monthly project status reports

➤ Project summary reports

High-level or summary project schedules are great when you have more than 100 tasks and want to provide executives with a snapshot of where the project is, from a schedule perspective. Executives rarely have the time to browse through a complex schedule with more than 100 tasks in it. Rather, a short summary explains matters far more clearly than a detailed schedule. The summary-level schedule should filter those tasks that are on a high level only. Figure 7.9 illustrates an example of a high-level summary schedule.

As the project manager moves forward on a project, information changes and progress updates are made to the baseline project plan and schedule. Whenever such progress

| ID | Task Name | Start | End | Duration | 2002 Jan | Mar/Apr | Jun/Jul | Oct | | |
|----|-----------|-------|-----|----------|----------|---------|---------|-----|---|---|
| 1 | Discovery analysis | 1/16/2002 | 4/9/2002 | 12w | | 100% | | | | |
| 2 | Equipment ordering | 3/22/2002 | 9/13/2002 | 25.20w | | | | 80.83% | | |
| 3 | Site installation | 9/13/2002 | 11/7/2002 | 8w | | | | 0% | | |
| 4 | Training | 8/1/2002 | 8/28/2002 | 4w | | | | 45.63% | | |
| 5 | Testing & Quality assurance | 9/19/2002 | 11/29/2002 | 10.40w | | | | 0% | | |
| 6 | Support and helpdesk | 11/25/2002 | 1/3/2003 | 6w | | | | 0% | | |

**Figure 7.9**   High-level executive summary

updates are made, it is wise to include these changes into the status report as well when reviewing a project or projects with the supervisor. Organizations usually have their own status report format that they would like to monitor, so it is important to understand what progress information to present. The following is some of the most common information that I have found project managers like to include in their project status reports:

➤ Project name

➤ Project number

➤ Project manager

➤ Client

➤ Contract amount

➤ Current project phase (e.g., SDLC phase)

➤ Upcoming tasks for the coming period

➤ Tasks or milestones completed

➤ Percentage complete

➤ Whether the project is ahead or behind time schedule

➤ Whether the project is over or within the cost schedule

➤ Number of change requests submitted since project start

➤ Corrective actions (if necessary)

➤ Risks and issues that require urgent attention

➤ Resource status

➤ A categorization system for the status report (e.g., the

color red for "in danger," yellow for "in trouble," and green for "OK"

Within many organizations, it is common to hold a general status report meeting where each project manager has the opportunity to report back to the group on the progress of each project. The group, in turn, has time to assist the project manager with possible solutions or ways to correct problems. I found this to work well at a cellular company; one project manager stated, "These meetings help me to resolve issues and risks that I didn't know how to solve. It helped me tremendously and also fostered a team spirit among my colleagues." It is just as common for status reports to be handled on a one-for-one basis with only the project sponsor or supervisor. So, it is necessary that project managers determine the type of status reporting that is required, the manner in which it is presented, and the frequency of these status reports.

## ■ LESSONS LEARNED FOR CONTROLLING THE PROJECT

➤ Motivate project team members and create incentives for teamwork.

➤ Deliver on promises to team members. Unfulfilled expectations can lead to negativity and poor performance.

➤ Never have arguments or conflict in front of others.

➤ Ensure that the project objectives have been clearly defined.

➤ Ensure that a risk management plan exists for any potential risk that may take place.

## PROJECT STATUS REPORT

Week Ending:_____

Project Number:_____     Project Manager :_____

Project Name:_____

Description:_____

Project Start:_____     Project End:_____     % complete:_____

☑ Check current Project Life Cycle Phase     STATUS ▶ G | Y | R

Concept | Planning | Design | Build | Training | Implement

### Project Documentation

Not started ☐
In development ☐
Revision update ☐
Sent for approval ☐

### Resources

Available ☐
Need to assess ☐
Need to hire ☐
Release resource ☐

### Equipment

Sent for approval ☐
On order ☐
Delivered ☐
Supplier paid ☐

### Project Issues/Risks

...........................................................................
...........................................................................
...........................................................................
...........................................................................
...........................................................................
...........................................................................
...........................................................................

**Figure 7.10**   Generic project status report

## ➤ Phase Completion Checklist

The project manager should ensure that the following project processes and documentation are implemented for this phase to be complete:

- ➤ A monitoring process
- ➤ Summary-level schedule for executive team
- ➤ Tracking schedule (GANTT chart)
- ➤ Certainty that the project team knows what to monitor
- ➤ Earned value spreadsheet (if required)
- ➤ Exception reports
- ➤ Updated project plan

# Chapter 8

# Implementing the Project

## ■ SUCCESSFUL IMPLEMENTATION: GETTING IT RIGHT!

Getting the implementation phase right the first time is crucial for any project manager or project team. This chapter offers guidelines for successfully implementing a project and ensuring that all relevant areas have been addressed. Remember that everything the project team planned, developed, and changed throughout the project life cycle is now ready for implementation. Implementation, in a nutshell, refers to the efficient transfer of the project into the client's "live" production environment. The logistical deployment of the project into the business operation is often complex and needs close coordination by the project team.

The users of the future system are anxiously waiting for the new solution and most probably have been briefed as to when the solution will be implemented and "up and running." If the production manager fails to deliver at the specified time and within the designed functionality, problems are bound to occur. There is no turning back! In this chapter I show how to implement a system and support it at a low cost. Failure to deploy a project correctly is one of the major causes of project failure. This chapter addresses the causes of poor deployment and highlights recommendations for a

243

successful one. The implementation of the solution is not final until sufficient attention is paid to ensure that client is knowledgeable and has been trained to use the solution. Training the client staff can take up considerable project resources, often a significant proportion of the overall cost of the project. Therefore, the training should be carefully planned and budgeted. The staff who will maintain and support the solution once it is implemented should also be offered training.

# ■ IMPLEMENTATION APPROACHES

There are a variety of options that a project manager could consider when implementing a solution. There are advantages and disadvantages to each type, and the choice usually depends on the client organizational setup and the complexity of the solution to be implemented. For example, an international client with multiple offices needs to upgrade a certain e-mail system in all offices by a certain "go-live" date. In such a scenario, a project manager is faced with huge logistical and technical challenges, and the implementation strategy is pivotal in deciding on the rollout. These implementation choices available to a project manager are

- ➤ Parallel implementation

- ➤ Phased implementation

- ➤ Crash implementation

## ➤ Parallel Implementation

A parallel implementation or approach implies that a new solution is implemented parallel to the current operational system in use. Those who are using the system will not see major downtime once it is implemented. The trick here is to implement the system. Once the new solution is tested and up and running, it is "switched" on and the older version is "switched" off. The advantages with a parallel implementation include (1) less disruption to the business, and (2) no loss of business if the new system suddenly fails.

## ➤ Phased Approach

Sometimes trying to implement a solution all at once is not feasible because many clients have essential operations that run during normal working hours and cannot afford the luxury of having their entire operation close down for a lengthy period in time. Often, clients have front office staff that attend to these operations (such as call centers, help desks, etc.), and they work in 24-hour shifts.

This is why many clients approve of a phased implementation approach, and the project team must ensure that the phased implementation is possible. This approach involves implementing the solution to a certain amount of users and then rolling them onto the new solution, while the rest of the users are rolled out in a similar fashion, until the entire solution is rolled out within the client environment. The phase approach works well because (1) there is minimal disruption to the clients operation, and (2) problems are resolved quicker.

The phased approach could also be used if there is more than one department. The project manager could decide that implementing the solution in one department at a time could be more reliable than trying to roll out all departments at the same time.

## ➤ Crash Implementation

Careful planning needs to take place when considering a crash (also known as full-blown) implementation. It takes an incredible amount of planning and re-planning to ensure no problems arise. In fact, with this type of implementation, the necessary contingencies need to be prepared and reviewed well in advance of the actual implementation, in order to minimize any potential failure. The necessary IT support staff also need to be available on the chosen implementation period. A full-blown implementation should be scheduled to take place over a slow period, such as a holiday or weekend.

## ➤ Implementation Checklist

The project manager must be sure that the implementation follows the implementation tasks and activities as stated in the project schedule. This forms the basis against which the implementation will be done. Generally, the tasks would be to

- ➤ Load or install the new system
- ➤ Perform a system test
- ➤ Convert to the new system
- ➤ Verify that an application works with other applications in the system
- ➤ Perform an integration test
- ➤ Perform an acceptance test

## ➤ The Implementation Plan

The implementation plan, which was developed by the project manager during the design phase, should, at this stage, be approved and communicated to all project stakeholders. A successful project can be ruined by a poor implementation plan. A working implementation schedule should be developed and maintained for all parties to use and agree upon. As the project changes, the project manager must pay close attention to the schedule and update it to reflect the latest changes to the implementation date. This schedule should then be communicated to all project stakeholders.

It is important to publish an initial implementation schedule for each site early in the project. Many members of the deployment project team will reach a point where they cannot until they know the time, sequence, or date of the implementation. Experience has shown that developing a draft implementation schedule early in the project life, rather than later, resolves many problems. The project manager should remember that the implementation plan could be put on hold if the software development is late for whatever reason. However, if the implementation plan cannot be moved and there is no slack in the schedule, the project manager should immediately escalate this risk to the necessary stakeholders.

### ➤ Meetings Leading up to Implementation

The implementation plan must be discussed and agreed upon by both the user management and IT support staff in order to ensure that both parties plan their work schedules to match the project schedule. For the majority of IT projects, implementation will most likely occur after hours or over weekends, during a series of working hours per day, or on public holidays.

## ■ QUALITY ASSURANCE

QA is often seen as an integral function that monitors and coordinates the quality used within the project management life cycle by evaluating the processes and procedures. Quality control, on the other hand, can be seen as a focused area (such as software testing) that compares the product to the specification or plan, with a focus of detecting and remediating errors or anomalies.

## ➤ The Role of QA on the Project

The person who is responsible for QA has many duties and responsibilities. The following section lists many of the things that a QA person would be expected to do.

- ➤ Participate in the change management process to assess the risk of putting fixes into the environment during acceptance testing.

- ➤ Assist the test team in isolating the source of discrepancies between expected and actual test results. If the error is in software design, thoroughly analyze the ramifications of any design changes. Design diagrams and structure charts before proceeding with corrections to code.

- ➤ Complete preparations for acceptance testing, including the establishment of the acceptance test environment. Unlike system testing, acceptance testing always takes place in the targeted environment. It is therefore extremely important to schedule computer resources well in advance.

- ➤ Check the simulated data to ensure that required test data have been produced.

- ➤ Obtain expected results from the acceptance test plan and review them for completeness.

- ➤ Calculate any missing expected results.

- ➤ Be certain that the introduction of new load modules is according to test configuration management procedures. When a new, corrected load module is received, first rerun tests that previously failed because of software errors. If these tests succeed, proceed with regression testing.

➤ Analyze and report test results. Evaluate test results as soon as possible after execution. Wherever possible, use automated tools in the analysis process. Record analysis procedures and keep all relevant materials. Remember that records and reports should give complete accounts of the procedures followed. If a test cannot be evaluated, note the fact and report the reasons for it.

➤ Compare all test results with expected results and note that all defects are documented, regardless of how minor they appear or whether they will be corrected.

## ■ PREPARING THE INFRASTRUCTURE

The planning for and preparation of the solution infrastructure prior to the actual implementation is an important step. Once the physical facility has been identified, the following aspects need to be managed by the project team:

➤ That sufficient power and workstations exist for all the users and equipment

➤ That sufficient workspace exists for all the identified users

➤ That network connectivity can be established between users and services or systems

### ➤ Equipment Setup and Configuration

It is important that the necessary hardware and software is (1) shipped, (2) delivered, (3) installed, and (4) configured correctly to reflect the requirements of the solution prior to the go-live date. The project manager needs to track and coordinate all IT equipment in support of the entire project implementation.

I remember a project that was performing a web site migration and had a certain go-live date, but failed to have the hardware delivery dates confirmed with the suppliers. The hardware was delivered six weeks behind schedule and the team had to make use of replacements until the ordered hardware arrived. This example clearly shows the importance of the managing the IT equipment necessary for implementation. Even delivery schedules must be confirmed from third party contractors to commit to the master project schedule.

### ➤ Networks Access to Users

Once the necessary solution is nearing the actual go-live date, the project manager should have a complete list of authorized users who will need access to the new system. This list is prepared prior to implementation because the task of obtaining user login passwords information can take time. The new IT solution should be configured to accept each authorized user of the new solution.

## ■ TRAINING THE CLIENT

### ➤ Training and Knowledge Transfer

Frequently, users of the solution are either not trained properly or they are not trained at all, which results in rejection of the solution within the client organization. It is important that users of the system receive all the training and support they need to use the new system effectively. The implementation of an IT system is not an end in itself. It is important that staff members are able to use it and that the impact of its introduction on their productivity has been fully considered during the planning stage. Without these considerations, is it is unlikely that the anticipated business benefits will be realized.

Training of staff can take up considerable resources, often a significant proportion of the overall cost of the project. Training must address the needs of users and of those operating and maintaining the system. The project manager has a few options when it comes to training resources on the developed solution:

➤ Outsource the training to a reputable, accredited training vendor.

➤ Provide the training in-house at the client.

➤ Provide the training at the project manager's organization.

Project managers need to realize that proper training must be provided to the users of the solution, and the following types of training can be provided before the solution is implemented and delivered for use:

➤ Classroom-based lectures

➤ One-on-one sessions

➤ Self-paced, computer-based tutorials

➤ Providing the user with an operations manual

Sufficient time and resources should be spent in order to help the staff learn how to use the IT system. Consideration should be given to the possible effect the new system may have on productivity in the period following implementation. In particular, it is important to make a realistic assessment of the impact that introducing the new IT system will have on the productivity and effectiveness of staff.

## ➤ Addressing the Training Infrastructure

Providing the training for users at a suitable training location is imperative in ensuring that the users are satisfied with the quality of the solution being implemented. If the training facility is situated at the back of the office, it immediately gives users the impression of an inferior solution. Sufficient thought and user acknowledgement must be given to training, and it starts by making sure that the users have (1) adequate training material, (2) training in a proper facility, and (3) the correct training resources. Using these three factors can only result in successful training.

Once training has been synchronized with the implementation schedule and approved by all the stakeholders, it becomes necessary that the system is tested and fully functional by the time that user staff return to their environment.

## ➤ Technical Support Training

Before implementing a project for a client, the project manager should be sure that the client IT operational support staff are adequately trained and knowledgeable on the technical support issues of the system being commissioned. After all, the IT support staff are responsible for maintaining the various technologies and platforms once the project is handed over. Table 8.1 displays the various levels of support that a project manager should discuss with the support staff prior to project implementation.

It is sometimes the project manager's responsibility to see that certain members of a client help desk operation (who deal mainly with technical queries and problems) are also provided with technical training to assist those individuals who may have problems with the newly commissioned

**Table 8.1**  Support levels that need to be accommodated

| Support Level | Focuses on |
|---|---|
| Level 1 | Basic setup and restoration of functions. Can be performed in-house. |
| Level 2 | Intermediate-level repairs within IT department. Can be performed in-house. |
| Level 3 | Complex technical support required with the solution provider/supplier. |

IT system. It is not always sufficient to provide only training for the client staff. Some of the necessary items to provide in addition to the training are

➤ Proper maintenance manuals, including checklists, for each level of support

➤ An approved and relevant service level agreement (SLA) contract between supplier/client

➤ An approved contingency plan

➤ Sufficient quantities of spare parts held for all critical items likely to fail

## ➤ Implementation Day

The implementation or go-live date for a new solution requires detailed planning, significant effort from both client and supplier, and the involvement of the stakeholders. The project manager leads this effort by bringing everyone together for the go-live date. The project manager should repeatedly check and double-check the implementation tasks and responsibilities prior to the go-live date until they are second nature.

It is not acceptable for the project manager to review the project schedule too late and accordingly arrange the initial go-live meeting on the actual date of implementation. This will not work. I cannot overemphasize here the importance of proper communication.

The project manager must understand that serious pressure to complete the implementation will result in business objectives being lost. The project manager must ensure that the processes for delivering the solution benefits include the following:

➤ The necessary project resources are available for the go-live dates.

➤ The schedule correctly reflects detailed project tasks and activities.

➤ The IT help desk is aware of the go-live date and has been briefed as to the possible volume and nature of calls that could be expected.

➤ A conference bridge telephone number has been reserved for everyone to use for the duration of the go-live date.

➤ The client is informed about the go-live activities and the role that the client will play in implementing the solution.

## ➤ Implementing over Weekends or Holidays

It is common to implement IT projects over quiet periods, such as weekends or even over holidays, in order to minimize any disruptions. The project manager must suitably plan the go-live period, and he or she cannot assume that it is the duty of the test team to prepare the next step in the implementation. The project manager should complete the following activities:

➤ Create and circulate a primary and secondary contact list of key implementation staff.

➤ Prearrange access to the facilities and IT systems.

➤ Establish a conference bridge number over the weekend or holiday. This can be scheduled at certain times or be staffed full-time.

➤ Consider opening up a status line. Regular voice mail project status can be left for all project stakeholders in order to brief them on the project progress.

➤ Once the project has been implemented successfully, send out the necessary success notifications.

## ➤ Risks and Issues to Consider

The following are early warning signs that the project might be going off track and is becoming a high risk:

➤ Tailored software enhancements (as opposed to minor customization of standard features) in the schedule of deliverables

➤ Any requests from a supplier or vendor for clarification, amendments, or deviations

➤ Stakeholders redefining any changes to the deliverables (scope creep)

➤ An unforeseen requirement for any specialist skills or resources

➤ Changing schedules without approval due to frequent slippage on progress reports

➤ No possibility of reverting to the "old" system in case of disaster

## ➤ Delivering What Was Promised

It is important that project managers deliver what was promised to the client, adding value wherever required. A readiness review is the formal transfer of information from the systems development team to the system test team. This process is to take place at the end of each phase of testing. The purpose of a readiness review is to communicate clearly the status of the system prior to the start of the system test. This is a critical step because it generates awareness of the following:

- ➤ The stability of each function

- ➤ Various tests that have been performed

- ➤ Outstanding defects (discussion of defects should take place)

- ➤ More functionality to be completed during the course of testing

## ➤ Acceptance Readiness Review

At the end of the system test phase, the project manager should conduct a readiness review meeting. He or she must meet with management, clients, members of the acceptance test team, and the development team to assess results of system testing and the state of preparations for acceptance testing. The output of the review should identify and discuss any outstanding problems that may impose technical limits on the testing or may affect schedules.

The system test and development teams should be certain that the system is complete and reliable before it is sent to the acceptance test team. Testers will be validating that business requirements have been fulfilled and ensuring integration into the target environment, so an accurate assessment of the status is necessary. A basic agenda for the readiness meeting would include the following points:

➤ A walk through of the functionality tested

➤ An estimated time of completion for any functionality to be finished during the next phase of testing

➤ A review of general design considerations

➤ A review of database design and business rules

➤ Outstanding problems that will not be fixed by the start of testing

➤ Outstanding problems that will not be fixed in the upcoming production release

➤ Changes (either additions or deletions) in the scope of the release

➤ A review of the current project plan

## ■ LESSONS LEARNED DURING PROJECT IMPLEMENTATION

"What could be simpler than buying some computers, throwing them on a desktop, plugging them in and turning them on?"

The question is simple: The answer is much more complex. Complexity is almost always underestimated until well after the start of the planning process. Many of the elements of deployment require special coordination and handling due to the lack of direct control over the processes or compounding dependencies. Complexity can come from the technical nature of a project that attempts to take advantage of a new technology not yet tested by the corporation and requires full integration into the existing systems. These factors don't surface until the project manager demands action or some form of change. Implementing a solution without testing it properly is not acceptable.

## ➤ I Wish I Had Known That

Look for early warning signs that planned business benefits will not be delivered.

- ➤ It is not clear that achieving the business benefits is the top priority of those managing the project.

- ➤ Time scales and resources for training, testing, and implementation support have been eroded by project slippage, and there are proposals to cut corners.

- ➤ Acceptance testing is being carried out by IS specialists and there is no involvement from the business.

- ➤ Other parties, who were not previously identified as part of the project, are now being identified as needing to be involved in acceptance testing and implementation.

- ➤ Staff involved in developing and agreeing to the original business objectives have moved on.

- ➤ The supplier has not demonstrated that the new system is compatible with existing systems and peripherals.

- ➤ The solution needs to be tested and demonstrated within the proposed environment (including links to existing systems). Have the tests for accepting the system from the supplier been planned and agreed upon? Has the process for data conversion been planned and has sufficient time been allowed for it?

➤ All necessary on-site preparations were not included in the planning (e.g., accommodation, cabling, safety, and security).

➤ All dependencies, such as slippage on other related projects, have not been taken into account.

➤ Too little attention is paid to testing the final solution.

## ➤ Phase Completion Checklist

The project manager should ensure that the following project documentation is filed within the main project folder in order to complete the project implementation phase:

➤ Project implementation plan

➤ Training plan and schedule

➤ Quality assurance plan

➤ Test cases and test scripts

➤ Acceptance certificate

➤ Status reports

➤ Minutes of the meeting

➤ Any inbound and outbound correspondence

➤ All final project costs, such as timesheets, invoices, and so forth

# Chapter 9

# Closing the Project

## ■ PROJECT CONCLUSION

Often the most neglected phase of any project is the closure phase. The closure phase brings the project to an orderly conclusion for the benefit of the organization and also for any future project. At this stage, the majority of project managers are looking at or have already been assigned new projects. It is exactly at this point that many project managers begin neglecting the closure phase tasks of a project. One of the main reasons for this is that there are administrative tasks to complete during this phase. However, it is important to remember that the *client* has paid for the project, and the *client* determines when the project is complete. So, remember to complete the project life cycle.

If the project does not receive the proper support until the very end, the client loses the benefits of the project and the project manager will most probably lose the recognition. In today's market, client satisfaction requires more than just implementing a quality solution. When a project is completed but the post-project support is not properly planned for, disaster strikes, leaving the client disappointed. This chapter not only shows how to review and close a project properly, but more interestingly, how to build a strong client relationship. So, when is an IT project really closed?

**Table 9.1**   Factors affecting project closure

| Factor | Authorized by |
| --- | --- |
| A decision is made stating that goals have been met. | Project sponsor and stakeholders |
| No additional value can be added to the project. | Project manager |
| Project handed off to operations (business). | Business manager or client |
| All resources have been released and reassigned. | Project manager |

Table 9.1 illustrates the various factors indicating a project coming up for closure.

Today, no organization can afford to throw away potential work that would benefit its strategy. Clients depend upon project managers being able to complete projects successfully. Project managers should realize that the project implementation phase does not, by default, imply project closure. The closure phase, in effect, implies that the project manager is ready to review the project, release the resources to the organization, and ensure that all documentation has been completed and finalized.

It is essential that organizations learn lessons from previous projects. There are many occasions where organizations require similar projects or technologies to be rolled out, and then find out, to their disappointment, that the previous project documentation was not archived or maintained. This poor practice of not maintaining a project history only wastes time. However, if the previous project documentation was archived and properly maintained (e.g., on-line library, project folder), this not only saves considerable rework for the project manager, but it lays the basic foundation for what may be ahead on the project. In essence, a sound practice of archiving, maintaining, and documenting the lessons learned on a project gives the project manager a head start.

A postimplementation project review is designed and held to establish the extent to which the organization has secured the business benefits they had desired. The review should include whether the project has met (1) business objectives, (2) user expectations, and (3) technical requirements. The project is normally rolled out to the operational business environment, which will be responsible for using the new system. Once this has been achieved, it is customary to have some form of celebration or acknowledgement to reward both project staff members and key stakeholders.

## ■ ADMINISTRATIVE CLOSURE

In order to complete the project closure phase entirely, it is necessary that the project manager complete all related project administration that was generated during the start of the project. This may be a contractual document that has not been obtained or, worse yet, outstanding payments that have not been finalized. Many project managers do not pay sufficient attention to the administrative aspect of the project as they often come out of environments where someone else does this work. In many projects today, it is up to the project manager to handle the administrative component. Remember that poor document management (e.g., poor filing practices, untraceable paperwork) will only create additional problems. The following section describes the minimum amount of administration necessary to prevent these types of problems from arising.

**Generate final project invoices.** All outstanding timesheets need to be submitted to the client for approval in order for invoices to be generated for payment. The reason being for this is that many resources such as consultants or vendors need final payment for certain equipment or services that were performed against the project. These costs need to be reviewed and processed before a project is closed. The project manager should confirm that the following have been reviewed and are correct:

➤ The original contract value has been fully invoiced.

➤ Any additional invoices are generated and submitted for project scope changes.

➤ All third parties suppliers and vendors have been paid as planned.

➤ Credit payments have been generated where applicable (e.g., penalties).

**Update the project folder.**   Most importantly, the project manager needs to update the project folder with all approved contractual documents before closing it off and sending it to the financial department or company archive for filing. The reason being is that the folder may be needed in the future for auditing purposes at the end of the financial year or for satisfying any future dispute or inquiry that may take place. The following content structure is recommended:

➤ The statement of work (SOW)

➤ Request for proposal (RFP)

➤ The client order or letter of intent

➤ Official correspondence on their company letterhead

➤ All invoices submitted to the client

➤ All credit notes submitted to the client

➤ Copies of time sheets submitted and approved

➤ Purchase orders generated on the project

➤ Subcontractor invoices and receipts for expenses

➤ Project disbursements made on the project (e.g., stationary, travel, etc.)

**Create the project review questionnaire.** This needs to be developed for the client in order to assess the overall success of the project from the client's perspective. This can assist the project organization in improving or correcting any areas that may need it—which may lead to additional training or process improvement.

**Create the project closure report.** It is customary to generate a professional report for company stakeholders on the findings of the client questionnaire. It should contain at least the following information:

➤ An executive summary

➤ A logical progression of the project—background, aim, and scope

➤ A brief description of risks—technical, financial, or resource

➤ Recommendations, if any

➤ Conclusions

➤ Acknowledgements that may want to be made

➤ Deliverable sign off

➤ Lessons learned—added to the project repository

➤ Client sign off

➤ Client reference letter

**Offer project recognition or rewards.** In many cases, it is customary to have a formal project "Hanover" ceremony or event, whereby stakeholders are rewarded or recognized. This may take the form of special certificates or flyers. These documents need to be coordinated (another project!) by the project manager. The following are examples of official rewards:

➤ Letter of Achievement or Acknowledgement to the stakeholder.

➤ Certificate of Friendship or Valued Relationship.

➤ A financial reward, in the form of a gift, voucher, or check

## ➤ Archiving Project Documentation

Because of the complexity and types of projects encountered, it is beneficial to archive project documentation and source code, in order to allow other project managers on future projects to review and use this archived media in a productive manner. This information can assist others by eliminating previously encountered problems.

New project managers will be in the position to leverage and develop extensions to historical project documentation with minimal disruption. If the same team is developing a similar type of project or solution, it is advisable to keep the documentation and lessons learned within that specific project team, and not move the information elsewhere. However, if the project information is incorrectly archived and improperly administered from a configuration or documentation management perspective, the following may occur:

➤ The information could be misplaced and cost valuable time being retrieved.

➤ The information could be lost permanently and hold no value to future projects.

➤ Only certain archived information will be recovered.

Similarly, if a project closes and much time passes before another project is considered, it is important to establish proper archive procedures so that the future project team can pick up where the last team stopped. I recommend that a centralized documentation and configuration management system be created to allow any future project teams to (1) identify, (2) control, (3) audit, and (4) account for historical project information. This information would include

➤ Development source code

➤ Project coding standards

➤ Project definition document

➤ Project charter

➤ Technical specifications

➤ Quality assurance plans and test scripts

➤ Minutes of the meetings

➤ Project management plan

➤ Master record index that lists all documentation placed under configuration control

➤ Project contact list

➤ Project notebook

It is imperative that someone makes and archives a permanent backup of the project information. Once the project manager has completed the "lessons learned" from the project, all project information must be sent to the repository (either manual or electronic based) for future referencing. This project archive repository should be managed by a (1) project office, (2) information systems configuration management department, or (3) an administration department. Archived project documentation should be classified and grouped by:

➤ Project type (e.g., Web applications/CRM)

➤ Project technology (e.g., Oracle)

➤ Project number (e.g., Project 12345)

➤ Financial year (e.g., 2002, 2003)

## ➤ Closure Checklist

I have always found that a closure checklist serves a useful purpose because it provides a quick summary of those project items that may require completion by the project manager. In order to achieve a proper closure on the project, the project manager should verify that the following questions have been answered.

➤ Have all the project objectives been achieved?

➤ Is the client satisfied with the overall project?

➤ Have the necessary post-project support agreements been established?

➤ What were the major concerns with the project?

➤ What are the key lessons learned from the IT project?

➤ What would you do differently?

➤ Do you feel the solution was cost effective?

➤ When would it be applicable to enhance or update the delivered solution?

## ➤ Early Project Closure

It may happen at any stage during a project that someone makes a decision to close down the project before it is complete. That doesn't sound too healthy, does it? The reason for this is most probably a culmination of bad events that lead to the project being closed: Project closure is rarely influenced by a single, random event alone. The decision to close the project is a large undertaking in itself and is normally made by the project sponsor and the executive team in the organization. Suffice it to say, closing a project early requires delicate handling, as the wrong approach will leave project team members disappointed and, in certain cases, leave the organization searching for other projects.

When closing down a project, the project manager should create a closure plan that names all the necessary resources and action items to remove and disassemble the project. A separate schedule will most likely be needed to perform an early closure, and the time scheduled to complete this should not be taken lightly. Any financial implications of the early closure of the project, such as penalties or losses, should be brought to the attention of the executive team.

Depending upon the circumstances of the specific project, it is wise not to rush in and blame individuals for the overall failure of the project. If the case is that the project manager failed to meet the project objectives, a decision should be made early on to replace the project manager, not to close the project.

## ➤ Communicating Project Closure

The central point of contact for project closure is the project manager, who (hopefully) by this time has proven his or her capability as an effective communicator. A project manager needs to provide effective feedback to (1) management,

(2) the client, (3) users, and the (4) project office about the progress on the final steps to completion. This is accomplished by having a project review meeting with the project office manager or direct supervisor. It is at this stage that management may present the project manager with another project or projects or inform him or her of an impending release.

Additionally, the project manager must also document the final project progress on the status report for the project file. The key here is to continue the communication process until the end of the project.

## ➤ Post-Project Review

A post-project review meeting should be held soon after project implementation, allowing both the client and the project manager to establish the extent to which they have secured the business benefits anticipated and to transfer any lessons learned (both positive and negative) back to future projects. The project manager calls this post-project review meeting and includes attendees representing the areas that are presented in Table 9.2.

Scheduling a post-project review meeting is often difficult; however, the project manager should announce the time well in advance and request all required team members attend. The project manager, when considering what to discus, should draw up a basic agenda and distribute it well in advance of the actual meeting. In particular, the post-project review meeting should seek to understand and document the following:

- ➤ Overall project status and highlights
- ➤ What the project risks were
- ➤ Lessons learned

**Table 9.2**  Post-project review staff

| Required Attendees | Optional Attendees |
|---|---|
| IS project manager | Project sponsor |
| Business project manager | Analysts, marketing, training |
| Client | Users, investors |
| Development manager | DBA, system administrator, developers |
| Software testing manager | Testers |
| Quality assurance manager | QA staff |
| Operations manager | Help desk, IT support |

➤ Reasons for cost overruns or cost savings

➤ Reasons for being behind schedule or ahead of schedule

➤ Scope creep and change control

➤ Resource utilization on the project

Reviews should be undertaken in a constructive and open manner with the aim of improving future project performance.

## ➤ Staff Reskilling

Investment in staff development is fundamental for any project's success. It is a known fact that information technology changes very rapidly (technologies from even three or five years ago may be inappropriate now), and on a large-sized project, individuals with outdated skills face a difficult time being selected on projects that require the latest skillsets. An example of this problem was transitioning from mainframe projects to web-based projects. Mainframe resources had to learn web-based skills quickly in order to secure work on future projects. The project manager, therefore, has an obligation to ensure that individuals have been trained in newer technologies in order to keep pace with today's global economy and time pressures. An emphasis on more formal and intense IT courses allows individuals to increase their learning pace and broaden their sources of information. The next project may very well be a project where trained individuals are able to assist.

# ■ RELEASING PROJECT RESOURCES

Once project staff members have finalized their respective tasks, they are to be systematically released back to the project "resource pool/consulting bench." In many cases, if the individual has impressed a client with fantastic technical skills, he or she probably will not be released. Instead, he or she will probably continue working with the client and be assigned a second project. Therefore, project managers should release their project staff in an orderly manner and provide individuals with advance feedback as to their next project or what the client is intending to do with them in the short term. If the individual is to remain with the client, the project manager should facilitate his or her re-utilization on other projects as soon as possible, if this is the intended plan. If the plan is not to use this person again, he or she is released back to the proper organization.

It is common practice that when individuals come off assignment and are released back to their organizations, they continue to book additional time to the project, and the project manager should communicate this fact to all individuals being released. If this situation is left uncontrolled, the project manager may face additional administration from the financial department, as the project may be billed for time not actually worked.

There are some definite advantages and disadvantages for those project organizations that release and draw their

**Table 9.3** Sharing a common resource pool

| Advantages | Disadvantages |
| --- | --- |
| Centralized resource pool | Best resources always on assignment |
| Ability to select technical resources | Remaining resources may be unsuitable |
| No external hiring necessary if resource is available | Underutilized resources |

technical resources from a common technical pool (see Table 9.3). If the project manager is releasing resources back to the resource pool, he or she should communicate this to the resource pool manager, who will start advertising the individuals' skills and capabilities.

# ■ MAINTENANCE AND SUPPORT

Once the project has been put through the acceptance testing trials, the system becomes the responsibility of the information systems support group either within the organization or within the company providing the support function for the organization. Support costs are not immediately visible to the client, and this is often where problems emerge. Clients will never be able to recover any system if the proper support infrastructure has not been put into place.

As an analogy for project support, I offer this example: The Brooklyn Bridge, long a symbol of "form meeting function," was an engineering marvel when it was constructed in 1884. Since then, this structure has undergone close to sixty major maintenance inspections and has been undergoing renovations since 1980—proving that even the soundest and most advanced designs need ongoing support. Whether it is construction or information technology, maintenance and support of systems need to be catered for and included into the life cycle for the client to review. Clients and project managers need to be aware of the full cost of the project life cycle once it is complete.

## ➤ Support after Project Closure

So often, projects are completed within time, specification, and cost and are formally signed off as successful project(s), but then fail dramatically within the coming few weeks and months, as a result of inadequate support being available for the implemented system.

Support can vary from solution to solution and really depends upon the complexity of the architecture being deployed. I have often seen solutions being handed over to clients who are so joyful at receiving the solution but who are ignorant about the full requirements and levels of support needed to maintain the solution. The project manager should contemplate the following questions when considering support and maintenance for a solution:

➤ Has the project manager involved the necessary IS support staff from the project start and has he or she made these staff aware of the architecture they are to maintain?

➤ Does the vendor offer 24x7x365 support and are the rates acceptable to the client?

➤ Are the approved SLAs developed and in place for each separate hardware and software item?

➤ Have the necessary software license fees per software seat been budgeted for an annual basis?

➤ Have the necessary hardware spares and accessories (which have a short life cycle) been ordered and placed into the store?

➤ Does the necessary hardware capacity and storage exist for future expansion of the system?

➤ Has sufficient bandwidth been allocated to handle calculated volumes of an intended solution?

➤ Has the IS support staff been trained in supporting the technology and are they able to resolve technical issues or able to contact the third-party suppliers for detail support?

➤ Has the help desk staff been trained to identify and log calls from users of the solution?

## ➤ Activating Help Desk Support

As proper customer relationships need to be managed during and after the project, it becomes necessary to ensure that the client IT help desk staff have been informed and have received the following aspects of the project, before closing off the project:

➤ The project manager has notified the help desk of the new solution, which is being accepted by the relevant business function (e.g., finance department).

➤ The help desk number is clearly displayed on the relevant application or specific web site, which users can contact.

➤ The help desk has received an updated contact list of details of the relevant internal staff, suppliers, and contractors who support the solution in any event of downtime or failure.

➤ The necessary operational support staff has been trained to the appropriate level of support to correct any technical problems that arise.

> ➤ The project manager has provided the help desk with a script of possible problems that users of the new solution could encounter.

## ➤ Service Level Agreements

The project manager and the operational support representative need to ensure that a formal service level agreement is developed and put into effect between the organization and suppliers, to maintain continued support and service.

## ➤ Future Upgrades and Enhancements

Isn't it ironic that the moment a project has been implemented, a magical list of enhancements and upgrades are waiting to be made to the project? Project managers should anticipate that the technology used on the implemented solution has a limited system life before it becomes outdated and thus requires enhancements or upgrades. In order to prepare for this eventuality, project managers should estimate when the next likely change will occur. They should forward these enhancements or upgrade costs and schedules to the operations manager or executive teams who are taking ownership of the live system. These forecasted costs should be placed on the medium- to long-term radar screen so as to assist with their budgeting and planning.

## ➤ Project Celebrations

If the project was successful, the project manager should hold a celebration for the project team. A celebration provides an excellent opportunity for the (a) project sponsor, (b) client, or (c) project manager to acknowledge specific individuals or team contributions, as well as present awards that may have been earned during the life of a project. A celebration brings closure to the project for all team members, and it serves as a motivation for the next project. In my experience, it is common to hand out project souvenirs or gifts to those members who achieved success.

## ➤ Project Management Forecast

In closing this chapter, I thought it most appropriate to forecast into the near future and envision the role that the IT project manager of tomorrow must play. Information technology projects are used in virtually every industry vertical today and will dramatically increase over the next few years, making remarkable achievements and strides in all industries. Yet, the phenomenon of information overload is in its infancy. By best accounts and predictions, if the amount of information doubles every eighteen months, then by 2010 there will be roughly 700 bits of data for every fact in existence. This does not necessarily imply that we will be better informed. As IT project managers, we will need to manage projects whereby meaningful facts—those that are useful and reliable—are put into place and then ensure that this information becomes a valuable resource.

Additionally, IT systems will also become far more powerful, intelligent, and flexible than ever before. Important changes will take place with such increasing frequency that it will become vital to manage the development and delivery of such solutions correctly. We will see rapid advances in the fields of (1) integrated web solutions, (2) telecommunications, (3) high-speed networks, (4) medical-based technologies, and (5) information engineering. These solutions may very well dictate that industries require new processes, integration, and functionality overnight. These are the types of challenges IT project managers will face in the near future.

Let me examine one of these verticals in closer detail. Projects in the medical and pharmaceutical industries will use an ever-increasing amount of information technology to

assist in identifying, diagnosing, and solving medical ill-
nesses. IT solutions ranging from noninvasive ultrasound
applications all the way to advanced applications, which
provide improved clinical capabilities, will be developed by
high-tech organizations to assist medical practitioners in
their daily tasks. These solutions will focus on utilizing su-
per-fast databases and analytical tools that can increase di-
agnostics techniques for studying medical data and can
allow for this complex data to be modeled and used to treat
patients. Together with the pioneers and visionaries out
there, project managers will still remain the key enablers in
designing, developing, and delivering a new generation of
applications and technologies to clients on a global basis.

The Human Genome Project is one of these kinds of projects. It applies the latest technology to shed light on how
faulty genes play a role in disease causation. The project,
which began in 1990, was originally scheduled to last fifteen
years, but it was completed way ahead of schedule, primarily
due to the rapid advances made in information technology.
The principles and application of sound project management were key in bringing this project within schedule. Interestingly enough, the technology objectives established at
that time were to:

> ➤ Identify all the 100,000 genes in human DNA

> ➤ Determine the sequences of the 3 billion chemical
>   base pairs that make up human DNA

> ➤ Store this information in databases

> ➤ Develop tools for data analysis

> ➤ Transfer related technologies to the private sector

# ■ I WISH I HAD KNOWN THAT

It is the project manager's secondary task, while working with the client site, to seek out and obtain repeat business where possible. Many opportunities are missed due to the fact that the project manager is eager to move onto other important clients in order to further his or her career and is not satisfied by remaining with a single client all the time. In doing this, the project manager loses valuable opportunities.

It is a common misconception that project closure is left until the very end in the project life cycle. In fact, it is catered for during the initial planning phase while the project manager is planning the entire project.

Be wary of those IT projects that are not formally closed and tend to drift and become subprojects. It is common for many organizations to simply extend the original project into yet another project where the initial "bugs" or trouble tickets can be resolved. In such a scenario, project members will easily become disheartened and will want to move onto something else. It is the project manager's job to ensure that the project is formally completed.

## ➤ Phase Completion Checklist

The project manager should ensure that the following project issues and documentation are completed and filed within the main project folder (e.g., manual or electronic) in order to complete the project closure phase:

- ➤ Project closure report
- ➤ Completed client questionnaire survey
- ➤ Project acknowledgements
- ➤ Final minutes of the meeting

➤ Any inbound and outbound correspondence

➤ All final project costs, such as time sheets and invoices (which should have been paid or collected)

➤ Final financial report

➤ Final technical report, including any patent(s) filed for during the project life cycle

➤ Inventory report of all project equipment—either leased or bought

# Glossary

**Accountability.** What a person can be counted on to do. That person will be called to account if the project he or she is accountable for is not achieved or does not meet the required standards.

**Activity.** A cohesive unit of work, the optimum level of reference for planning and communication.

**Architecture.** The software architecture includes the data model structure, user interfaces, workflow, and interactions of the various components. It is the blueprint for the design of the software project.

**Bar chart.** A graphical representation of activities within a project over time. The duration of each activity is shown as the bar, the ends of which correspond to the start and end dates of the activity. A bar chart is also known as a Gantt chart.

**Baseline.** An element of the business case for a project describing costs and performance levels that would be achieved if those operations continued unchanged over the planned period of the project. The baseline is used to compare the costs and benefits of the options evaluated in the business case.

**Business analyst.** An individual who performs the business assessments and improvements to an organization's products or systems.

**Business case.** The section of the project definition statement that provides the justification for the commitment of resources to a project. The business case should demonstrate that the most cost-effective combination of projects has been selected when compared with cost alternatives. It also provides the wider context and justification for infrastructure investment and costs of implementing policies and standards.

**Business operations.** A grouping of one or more business processes that combine to achieve a primary goal of the organization (for security benefit).

**CCB.** See *change control board.*

**Change control.** A formal process through which the changes to the project are introduced and approved.

**Change control board.** Steering committee established in order to approve or reject proposed changes to a system or product. The CCB may require further assessments and feasibility before making a decision.

**Change request.** A process that details a proposed change, evaluates the change, makes a decision to approve or reject.

**Closure.** Formal end to the project, either because it is completed or because it has been prematurely ended.

**Communications plan.** The plan for how the objectives, plans, and progress of the project are to be communicated to staff in order to promote a feeling of common ownership, to facilitate knowledge transfer and training, and to ensure that those staff are involved throughout the life of the project.

**Concept phase.** The second phase of project management. A feasibility study is conducted to explore options for realizing the benefits framework described in the Program Brief. The program is fully defined, a benefits management regime established, and funding approval for major projects is obtained. Initial Project Briefs are written that specify project deliverables and outline project plans. The results of the phase are documented in a Program Definition Statement.

**Configuration management.** Approach to identifying, controlling, and auditing all system items that may be affected by fit, form, or function.

**Contract.** A mutually binding agreement that obligates the supplier to provide specified products and services to the buyer, who must pay for them.

**Corrective action.** Actions taken, upon evaluation of gaps between performance and plan, to remedy the gaps and put the project back on track to deliver.

**Cost Benefit Analysis.** A project technique for comparing the costs of taking a particular course of action with the benefits achievable from the outcome.

**Cost control.** The controlling of all changes to the project budget and its re-forecasting.

**Cost monitoring.** The tracking of the costs spent to date on the project and forecasting the costs likely to spend.

**Cost variance.** The cost difference of project activities. The variance can either be positive or negative.

**Critical path.** The sequence of project activities that determines the earliest completion time for the overall project.

**Deadline.** The final date or completion date for a specific activity or milestone.

**Deliverables.** The specific outputs that the project seeks to deliver. They are tangible benefits that people can see. Each key deliverable is defined as a milestone on the project plan.

**Dependency.** Project activities that are linked or connected to other project tasks. One task cannot be completed or started until the other has been started or completed.

**Design authority.** A role within the project that has the responsibility to manage the design of the business and information systems that are affected or created by the project. This means ensuring that designs are consistent across all projects in the portfolio and consistent with supporting services and infrastructure designs and plans, and that designs comply with the policies and standards of the organization and the project. The design authority is also responsible for change control to technical specifications and technical infrastructure.

**Development plan.** A formal plan describing the details of the software development on the project.

**Duration.** The total period of time from the start up of an activity to its completion. This period of time typically consists of the time required to move the work to completion.

**Earned Value.** A performance-based management system for establishing baseline cost, schedule, and performance goals for a capital project and measuring progress against these goals.

**Effort.** The actual time required to complete a project activity.

**Estimate.** An analysis or forecast of the proposed activities, efforts, and resources to be utilized on a project.

**Feasibility assessment.** During the Project Definition phase, the project feasibility study is conducted to develop in further detail the business requirements and benefits analysis contained in the Project Brief in order to draw up the *blueprint* of the future business operations and to scope and structure implementation options.

**Gantt chart.** Simple technique for displaying the schedule of activities or tasks against a time line and identifying the critical path within a project.

**Go / No Go Decision.** A formal decision that is made by a committee or executive to commence with or cancel the project.

**Goal.** The desired end result. It can be defined as a specific measurable accomplishment to be achieved within a specified time and cost constraint.

**Identification phase.** The first phase of project management, in which all high-level change proposals from available strategies and initiatives are considered collectively and their objectives and directions translated into one or more achievable projects of work. For each project identified, a Project Brief is written and a project director appointed.

**Implementation plan.** A plan describing how the project is going to deliver and approach the implementation of the proposed changes.

**Implementation strategy.** The overall approach to be used in implementing a change into the business or market.

**Information technology.** Electronic-based computer systems, appliances, and software.

**Infrastructure.** In this guide, infrastructure is broadly defined to include both "traditional" forms of infrastructure such as IS/IT, telecommunications, and estates, as well as supporting services such as accountancy, staffing, and personnel.

**Issues.** Those specific items that have occurred and may threaten the success of the project.

**Issue log.** A record of all issues relevant to the project that, if left unresolved, could have a negative effect on the project.

**IT.** See *information technology.*

**Kick-off meeting.** An initial meeting held with project stakeholders to discuss and present project goals, scope, and responsibilities.

**Life cycle.** A sequence of defined phases over the full duration of a project. Each phase has specific characteristics and each forms part of a logical sequence in which the deliverables are defined and created.

**Linear responsibility chart.** A technique used to identify, isolate, and document various roles and responsibilities within a project or program.

**Methodology.** A process established that can be adhered to in order to meet objectives.

**Milestone.** This specifies the results or condition that a project must occupy at a particular point in time in order for the project to remain on track to achieve the project goal.

**Milestone plan.** A summary of the project milestones and corresponding dates.

**Monitoring.** This involves the process of capturing, assessing, and reporting on project performance as compared against the plan.

**NPV.** See *net present value.*

**Net present value.** A technique based upon the principle that a given sum of money is worth more today than in later years. Allows project manager to reduce all values, both costs and benefits, to a single sum expressed in today's money.

**Network diagram.** Schematic display of the project's activities and the logical relationship (dependencies) between them. Also referred to as the Arrow Diagramming Method (ADM) as each arrow represents an activity.

**Phase.** A part of the project's life cycle, into which activities to manage the project are grouped. The main phases of the project are Concept, Planning, Execution, Control and Closure.

**Projects In Controlled Environments** (the CCTAs standard methodology now called PRINCE 2) is used for project management by many government and large, private-sector IT departments. Now designed to make the method more suitable for smaller and non-IT projects.

**Procurement plan.** Formal plans listing the resources that need to be purchased for the project.

**Project.** A single, temporary set of activities bounded by a business objective. The project includes the controlled environment of management responsibilities, activities, documentation, and monitoring arrangements by which the portfolio of projects achieves its goals and the broader goals of the program.

**Project definition.** The agreed statement of objectives and plans between the target business operation, the project director, and the senior management group (management board, steering committee) to whom the Project Director is reporting. This forms the basis for funding the project and is the key monitoring and control document. It is a dynamic document, maintained throughout the life of the project.

**Project director.** The senior manger with individual

responsibility for the overall success of the project. This person is drawn from the management of the target business area.

**Project execution phase.** The third phase of project management, in which the project portfolio management and transition activities are undertaken. Compliance with the project design, corporate and project policies, standards, and infrastructure plans is monitored and assured.

**Project folder.** A collection and categorization of key project documentation accessible to project stakeholders during and after the life of a project. A hardcopy file or electronic folder is maintained.

**Project management plan.** The approved working master document used on a regular basis by the project manager and his or her team to identify, monitor, and track the development of the project.

**Project manager.** The appointed person who is responsible for the day-to-day management of the project, on behalf of the organization.

**Project office.** See *project support office.*

**Project review.** A formal review of the project at a certain point in time. Determines the progress made, risks, issues, and general trends. Can be held at each phase of the project.

**Project support office.** An organization rendering the necessary administration to the project manager, particularly with management information reporting. This office may, where appropriate, serve both the program and the individual projects.

**Project templates.** A series of standardized electronic or hardcopy formats used on the project.

**Prototyping.** The development of a product or solution through the creation of rough mock-ups, which through trial and error, get increasingly closer to the desired end result.

**QA.** See *quality assurance.*

**Quality assurance.** The planning, design, work, and procedures necessary to ensure that the necessary quality is achieved.

**Quality control.** The inspection of finished products to ensure that they meet the required standards or are fit for their purpose.

**Quality plan.** A component of the Program Definition Statement that sets out quality objectives for the program's design and execution, for the future business as described in the *blueprint,* and for managing third parties involved in the project.

**RAD.** See *rapid application development.*

**Rapid application development.** A technique used to facilitate and increase the development of an application.

**Request for proposal.** Used as a bid document to solicit proposals from suppliers in a format that facilitates comparison and ensures sufficient clarity on what is being requested.

**Resource plan.** A component of the project definition statement that addresses how the project will be resourced and specifies what supporting services, infrastructure, and third party services are required.

**Resource pool.** A list of resources available for assignment to a task or group of tasks for multiple projects.

**Return on investment.** Formal technique used to calculate the project's financial return based upon the initial investment.

**RFP.** See *request for proposal.*

**Risk.** Any potential threat or occurrence that may prevent the project from being successful. A risk is an event that may happen.

**Risk plan.** A component of the project definition statement that contains a record of all risks in the project environment. It assesses possible impact and describes what is to do (and when) to avoid, remove, and control risks. It includes the detailed processes for managing the risk.

**ROI.** See *return on investment.*

**Schedule.** A timeline that shows when a project is to be completed.

**Schedule variance.** The calculated schedule difference indicating whether the schedule is ahead or behind schedule.

**Scope.** Establishes the boundaries within which the project will work and helps define the areas it will effect.

**Service level agreement.** A contractual document detailing the level of work and the work schedule to be performed by the vendor. The SOW becomes part of the eventual contract between the vendor and the organization.

**SLA.** See *service level agreement.*

**SME.** See *subject matter expert.*

**SOW.** See *statement of work.*

**Sponsor.** Person accountable to the business for the achievement of the project goals and benefits. The sponsor achieves this through the project manager and project team.

**Stakeholder.** Anyone who has, or believes he or she may have, the right to be involved in the project. Stakeholders are affected by the project; they are either interested in the progress of the project or are the actual users of the proposed solution.

**Statement of work.** A formal document created by an organization in response to an RFP that describes the tasks to be completed in sufficient detail.

**Status report.** Project progress, variance, and corrective actions are summarized by project mangers in brief status reports. These are collated by a project office into a project progress report, which is issued prior to each Project Executive meeting. Status reports should cover forecasts of problem areas as well as overall project performance.

**Steering committee.** A body established to monitor the project and to assist the sponsor and project manager in overseeing the project and delivering the benefits.

**Strategy.** A formal plan indicating the course of action to be undertaken to maintain a competitive edge.

**Subject matter expert.** An individual having specialist knowledge in those areas required by the project.

**Supplier.** An organization rendering a service or products to the project in support of meeting the project goal

**SWOT.** An analytical technique to help develop a plan based upon different internal and external factors for an organization or marketplace. Known as Strength, Weakness, Opportunities, and Threats analysis.

**Systems analyst.** An individual who performs a technical assessment and analysis to an organization's products or systems.

**Task.** The smallest indivisible part of an activity that is needed to track a project.

**Team.** A group of people who need to achieve complex tasks and mutual goals that require creativity and interdependent work to succeed.

**URS.** See *user requirements statement.*

**User requirements statement.** A formal project document detailing the exact client requirements demanded for the project.

**Work breakdown structure.** A technique that provides a logical format for organizing all the work required to deliver a project. Visually, the work breakdown structure can be compared to an organizational chart. The first layer is the project goal, the second layer is the milestones, the third layer is activities, and the fourth layer is tasks.

**WBS.** See *work breakdown structure.*

# Index

# ■ ABOUT THE AUTHOR

Jason (Jay) Charvat is an accomplished consultant Project Management Professional in the fields of Systems Engineering and Information Technology, where he completed many successful projects in the Defense, Logistics, Manufacturing, Publishing, Governmental, Pharmaceutical, Cellular and Telecommunications industry verticals. He has extensive knowledge on project methodologies, project processes, and practical techniques used in the completion of projects. He is a certified consultant and has consulted regularly throughout the US. He is a member of the Project Management Institute (PMI). He holds a BS (Information Sciences) degree in addition to numerous professional qualifications from the United Kingdom. He has served as a commissioned Airforce captain, specializing in the information technology environment. Jay serves as a project management consultant and senior manager for RCG Information Technology, Inc., in New Jersey. He can be reached at jaycharvat@hotmail.com or www.jasoncharvat.com.

Lightning Source UK Ltd.
Milton Keynes UK
UKHW041638080219
336977UK00001B/37/P

9 780471 139263